California Trout

CALIFORNIA
TROUT
JIM FREEMAN

The Complete Guide to Trout Fishing in California

Chronicle Books
SAN FRANCISCO

Library of Congress Cataloging in
Publication Data
Freeman, Jim.
California trout.
Consists of revisions of California
trout fishing, How to catch California
trout, and North Sierra trout fishing.
Includes index.
1. Trout fishing—California.
2. Fishing—California—Guide-books.
I. Title.
SH688.U6F73   799.1'755   81-21749
ISBN 0-87701-251-2   AACR2

Editing: Thomas Miller
Design: John Beyer
Layout: Michael Fennelly
Composition: Type by Design
Cover photographs: R. Valentine
   Atkinson

Chronicle Books
275 Fifth St.
San Francisco, CA 94103

10   9   8   7   6   5   4

Contents

California Trout

California Trout Fishing

In introducing this guide to California trout fishing it was my idea that perhaps California trout fishermen were missing the boat when it comes to enjoying and understanding what an outstanding place California is for the trout angler. Californians are noted as the most travelled anglers in the world. During the seasons spots in Montana, Idaho, Utah, British Columbia and many other places are literally overrun with anglers from California. But I have a hunch that when the serious trout fisherman gets some hint of just how productive selected California fishing waters are, many will choose California for a great deal of their trout fishing.

I have personally fished virtually every major area in the west for trout and other species. In some respects certain other spots are superior to California trout fishing (as in the case of stream fishing in the eastern part of Montana, or some of the high mountain lakes in Utah and other spots). However, when you consider all of the things that go to make up a trout fishing trip, California has much to offer. California has good trout fishing for the fishing members of the family, plus other kinds of outdoor enjoyment for the non-fishing members of the family. And for the length of the season that the fisherman can practice the game, California does not take a back seat to any other western trout fishing area.

Why this Guide?

In this guide I am trying to set out an ethic of trout fishing that is suited particularly to California fishing conditions and the species of trout found in our waters.

In my travels throughout the state I have found the vast majority of anglers are simply doing the wrong things when they fish California waters. In many cases this is because anglers have come to California from states where other techniques are productive. These techniques simply fail to produce in California waters.

We have some unique situations in California trout fishing, rarely if ever duplicated in other areas. A perfect example is our reservoir systems. Where originally we had 38 stream systems flowing freely to the ocean we now only have three major streams that are primarily free flowing. In a way this a loss, but the reservoirs exist so we may just as well learn to fish them properly for trout.

Trout Guide Contents

With this trout fishing guide I will assume that the reader has at least a rudimentary knowledge of how to rig trout fishing tackle and how to use it in a proper way under most circumstances. This guide is not really intended as a trout fishing primer. Rather, it is intended to be a specific guide, as complete and accurate as possible, to trout fishing at specific spots. There will be material presented here that is technical in nature when I feel that it is necessary or practical so that the reader can get the maximum benefit out of his fishing time.

Length of Season

A serious California trout fisherman can find really high quality trout fishing for twelve months of the year. California is, after all, a thousand miles long from north to south. Within this length of climatic variation you find ideal conditions for trout fishing year around.

California not only spans an immense variety of weather and climate zones but it also offers trout fishing from sea level to an elevation of around 10,000 feet. This means that there is not really a single peak to our trout seasons. In California, by heading north or south or by heading for different elevations the angler can find peak fishing conditions all year.

Accessibility

The unique feature of California waters is the large percentage that is readily accessible to fishermen. Unlike trout waters in many of the western states, Canada and Alaska, you can drive up to most of our significant trout areas. Many anglers do not consider this a benefit. They maintain this easy access has cut into the quality of trout fishing as a sport.

I disagree with much of this kind of thinking. I see little charm in a situation where you know there is good fishing in a stream, or stream and lake system, but it is located so far back in the woods an expensive and often grueling trip is required just to get to the water's edge. I have found many streams located right next to a highway can produce fine

This is what it's all about when it comes to trout fishing. The lakes and streams in this guide can be some of the finest fishing water in the west for the angler who goes about fishing them in the right way. Fighting trout of large size can be taken at will by the angler who learns the right spots to do his fishing and then uses the proper techniques.

catches of trout. All that is necessary to enjoy this kind of fishing is learning a few techniques that are rarely used by the majority of anglers fishing these streams.

Anyone who wants virgin fishing can find plenty of it in the extremely high mountains of California. There are literally hundreds, if not thousands, of tiny lakes and stream systems in our mountain areas where a fisherman can find all the solitude he could wish for. In order to enjoy this facet of the trout fishing game all an angler needs to pay is the chore of hiking in or making the trip to wilderness waters on horseback.

I have chosen the spots that we are covering in this guide with several things in mind. The streams named are very accessible to the general public. The settings are classic and the fishing is of superior quality.

The lakes chosen are also very accessible and if there is a fee charged, the amount is very modest and well within the budget of any angler. All the waters in this guide are located within easy driving range of major metropolitan population centers, and most can be reached in an automobile. The exceptions are a few in the high country north of Tahoe, which were included for the angler who either has a four-wheel-drive vehicle or likes to hike a bit for better sport.

Reservoir Systems

In California trout fishing an angler has to learn how to deal with the factor of altitude if he is going to be consistently successful. The altitude factor is extremely important because of the significant reservoir systems on our major streams. A typical example would be the one found on the Feather River. The lowest reservoir on this river that can be fished for trout is the Forebay and Afterbay below Oroville Dam. There are many other reservoirs in this single drainage up to extremely high altitude.

In fishing massively dammed rivers like the Feather, Sacramento, San Joaquin, Bear, Yuba, and many other streams, the angler who fishes lower elevation reservoirs in the spring, then fishes higher lakes as the season progresses, can find prime fishing conditions all year long. As fall turns to winter the angler should again start fishing down to lower altitudes if he wants to get prime fishing.

In California you can consider a fishery a trout fishery any time you fish above a large reservoir. Even though these upstream trout often (maybe always) migrate to res-

Good trout can often be taken in very small streams. Many anglers overlook these spots because they think they are overfished.

ervoirs for a large portion of their lives, they can still be considered true to the ethic of trout fishing.

Fishing Streams

In most cases massive damming has done harm to trout fishing in California. Where once we had thousands of miles of natural streams we now have to learn what irrigation districts and utilities have done with the water in the remaining miles of our streams.

In many cases you will find streams that were minor creeks or rivers before damming have become major trout waters simply because the damming agency now uses them to transport water to downstream facilities. In other cases streams that once were major trout producers now have a meagre flow of water hardly capable of supporting a large trout population. The trout fisherman who wants to be successful should be aware of factors such as stream water manipulation because they can be critical influences.

Limits in Technique

There are many relatively unused methods of taking trout that are es-

pecially effective in California trout waters. These are the techniques we'll be working with.

In California trout fishing there are so many different situations that at one time or another an angler who fished the entire state for trout would find need for every type of equipment ever designed for trout fishing. But in this book, I won't delve into subjects such as the deepline wire trolling equipment used only for lake trout (mackinaws) in the two lakes that have this species.

California Trout Fishing Is Great!

To sum up. Fishing for California trout can be great if you make the effort to learn how and where to catch them. No single method or way of fishing will work in all our streams. But a combination of different factors, once understood, can make California trouting as good as that found anywhere in the country.

Equipment for Trout Fishing

Any fishing trip starts with the selection of fishing equipment suitable for the conditions you will find on the lake or stream. Generally, the clarity of the water will determine what kind of rigging and terminal equipment is required, but in California trout fishing an angler will meet with many different situations. Perhaps an outline of the equipment I use and the ways I use it will be of value to the reader. My own equipment is very probably much more extensive than that used by the average fisherman, but then, I probably fish a great deal more than most anglers.

Spinning Equipment

The Reel

The reel is the heart of any spinning outfit. The rod and line play a far less important role.

The most important thing about the spinning reel that you choose is that it should have a quick change feature so you can change spools of line in a hurry.

A good modern spinning reel can be bought in most larger cities for less than $50. This is well within the reach of most anglers. The best reel for all-around fishing is the standard open-face model. I use a Mitchell 300 for most of my trout fishing. This reel is probably the most popular in the American fisheries.

This popularity is an important item in reel selection. An angler should choose a popular model and make of reel; then, if something goes wrong with the reel while on a fishing trip, it can be repaired in even the smallest town. If an angler chooses a reel that is not common he can often ruin a trip because the only place it can be fixed is in bigger cities away from trout fishing areas. Reels from any of the larger companies are suitable for California trout fishing.

The Rod

The key to rod selection is to purchase a rod that is limber enough to handle a variety of lines yet with enough backbone to handle heavier lines.

The 7-½ ft. rod (Fenwick FS 75) I use is very limber. I have found that for consistent success I get bet-

Spinning equipment can be used effectively on larger streams like the Truckee or the north fork of the Feather River. Good browns can be found in both streams.

ter results with a rod that bends right down into the handle section. As a matter of fact, I don't like the feel of any rod that doesn't have some give in the handle section at the spot where I have my hand. This makes the rod an extension of your arm and you can sense every move that the trout makes as he makes it.

Lines

Probably the best all-around line size for California trout waters is four-pound test monofilament. This size line can be rigged to cast fairly light weights and is strong enough to handle virtually any trout likely to be hooked, providing the angler doesn't panic. A spool of six-pound and eight- and ten-pound test should also be purchased. If economy is a factor select four-, eight- and twelve-pounds as line sizes for various spools.

Extra Spools of Line

One of the reasons for an open-face reel is the ease with which spools can be changed. Closed-face spincasting reels are difficult to adapt in the field; therefore, an angler is likely to change from one line size to another to cover a changing situation. Also, the closed reel keeps the line spooling hidden. When something goes wrong with the line, as when a loop or slippage happens, an angler with a closed reel doesn't see the trouble as it develops. By the time he is aware of a tangled line the situation is often hopeless. With an open-face model trouble with the spooling line can be spotted with a glance down at the reel spool.

In my own fishing I have two spinning rigs fitted and ready to go at all times. One rig is fitted with relatively heavy line for trout fishing that tests around 8 or 10 lbs. breaking strength. The other is fitted with 4 or 6 lb. test monofilament.

One reason for having two outfits: I have found the best method of locating trout in lakes like Davis or Eagle is to troll, but once they are located it is usually better to cast to them with a lighter outfit.

But in stream fishing, as it is done in streams like the McCloud and Sacramento, I need only the lighter outfit, normally fitted with 4 lb. test line. This rig will handle the smaller and lighter lures needed for success in these clear water streams. Heavier gear is almost surely ruled out in these streams except during the spring or rainy period when the waters are roiled. In the case of the McCloud River I have never seen this stream roiled more than modestly, even during storms.

Ultra-Light Lines

There will be some situations in California trout fishing where very light lines are a distinct advantage. It is good sense to buy 100-yard spools of one- and two-pound test lines for these occasions. I don't suggest filling a special spool with lines this light. Instead, when a situation arises where very light lines are warranted, simply wind on about 50 yards of the lighter test line over the top of the four-pound spool. Rarely will you need more than this much line. On a properly maintained standard-size reel the drag can be adjusted so it can handle this size line effectively.

Here is a key to success in trout fishing. Having a selection of spools with different size lines (and loaded correctly) will allow the angler to change techniques in a very short length of time. It's cheap insurance to have these spools.

The situations where lines less than four pounds are advantageous are fairly limited. In summer most streams in California run extremely clear. They are also relatively shallow in many sections. With light lines an angler can handle very tiny lures like midget spinners and wobblers that are deadly in stream and lake fishing without any additional weight added to the line. In a few situations lines of one-pound test will be necessary but I consider two-pound test the minimum for the majority of situations. Lines lighter than two pounds are violently affected by even the slightest breeze and trying to fish them where there is any brush is a nuisance.

There is very little advantage to using the tiny rods commonly associated with ultra-light fishing. Perhaps these short rods, normally about four feet long, can be used to advantage in brush stream fishing but they do not allow enough line control in most cases to justify their purchase—unless the angler just likes the idea of fishing with a tiny rod. I just use my regular 7- or 7½ ft. rod.

Fly-Fishing Equipment

It's a good idea when choosing fly-fishing equipment for California trout fishing not to choose outfits extremely light or too heavy for the work they are to do. I get more use out of my FF 70 and FF 80 Fenwick rods than all the others I own. These, or rods like them, are about in the middle range of the company line. They can handle lines suitable for all California situations. The rod, at any rate, is one of the least important factors about fly fishing. The important thing is to fit a proper line to whatever rod is chosen to get a combination that works well for your particular type of casting.

Fly Line Fit

The line-to-rod fit is indicated for all the better rods on the market today. Some, like the Fenwicks, even have the proper line size indicated on the butt of the rod.

The numbers and letters in this line designation for line-to-rod fit are based on the standards set by the American Fishing Tackle Manufacturers Association (AFTMA). These standards refer to the number of grains of weight in the first 30 feet of the fly line. The letters refer to the type of line taper and the floatability of the individual line:

AFTMA Fly Line Standards

No.	Wt.	Range (Manufacturing tolerances)
1	60	54– 66
2	80	74– 86
3	100	94–106
4	120	114–146
5	140	134–146
6	160	152–168
7	185	177–193
8	210	202–218
9	240	230–250
10	280	270–290
11	330	318–342
12	380	368–392

AFTMA Fly Line Symbols

L = Level
DT = Double taper
WF = Weight forward
ST = Single taper

AFTMA Fly Line Types

F = Floating
S = Sinking
I = Intermediate
(Float or sink)

Fly line-to-rod fit is so essential to good fly fishing that an inexperienced fly fisherman should choose only rods that have line sizes predetermined. Most fly line companies publish charts to show which lines fit popular rods on the market. The lines I use—Scientific Angler, Sunset and Gladding—are standards of the trade. They all make good lines for trout fishing.

Fly Leader

I consider the fly leader the most important element in fly fishing for trout. A properly designed leader that turns over a fly perfectly at average casting distances is actually as important as the fly being used. A fly that doesn't turn over on the cast, or that arrives with a splash, will take few of our sophisticated trout.

It is actually impossible for one angler to design a leader for another fisherman. Every angler casts a little differently from another fisherman. Each fisherman should work with his leader until it is performing right for him, rather than relying on a general leader design outline. I have tried commercial leaders that are pre-tapered but have generally had to alter them so much to suit my own standards that it made little sense to pay the additional price for them.

There are three things to keep in mind when selecting monofilament for leaders. The diameter of the leader material is critical. The

*Fly fishing equipment that is rigged properly is probably
the most effective gear to use for taking trout in the streams of
California. Often one has to taper leaders down to 1 pound test
in order to score in extremely clear water.*

stiffness of the material is important and the breaking strength of the knotted line is important. Odd as it may seem I tested many different brands of monofilament and found the test of the line on the spool had little to do with the actual strength of the line on the spool. Because of this the only way you can properly design a leader is to rely on the diameter of the line. Good brands of line will have this measurement on the spool label.

Leader Design

A good leader should have approximately two-thirds of its length of comparatively heavy monofilament. The next section should be short and made of line that differs no more than .003 between sections. Lines with more than this much difference in diameter are almost impossible to tie together.

There is no way to discuss the stiffness of monofilament. What is stiff to one person is not to another. However, it's a good idea to check the various lines against each other when working out a leader. For dry fly work I use stiffer line in the butt section and limper lines for sections closer to the fly. The tippet section should always be as stiff as you can find. This stiffness tends to turn the fly over cleanly, a very important element in proper delivery of the fly.

Leader Construction

In order to give the beginner a basis to work from I'll give the formula I use for building the basic leader. I don't look at a leader the same way others do. To me the basic leader is the different sized lines used to get the thick butt section tapered properly down to the size of the tippet section. To me the tippet is not really a part of the rest of the leader. The tippet length determines how well the fly is delivered.

A tippet that is too long for an individual fly will not let the fly turn over right. One that is too short will allow the fly to turn over with a splash. This is not necessarily always a liability. Often, when stoneflies and larger caddis are on the water you want the fly to arrive with authority. A stonefly will hit the water with a splat that is audible for quite a distance. When trout are feeding actively on stoneflies they suspect anything that arrives quietly. In general, though, you want a fly to arrive on the water with as little commotion as possible.

For some reason, it has become a tradition to have two sizes of leaders, 9 feet and 7½ feet in length. I think this is foolish. There is nothing sacred about leader length. If you can handle a 15-foot leader, it is almost always to your advantage to do so, particularly on smooth flowing streams and all lakes. If a leader is properly designed and the caster has any talent at all with his casting, he should take advantage of his ability.

Here is a standard leader that works well for me with a floating line on my rods: 36 inches of .020; 32 inches of .018; 8 inches of .016; 8 inches of .014; 6 inches of .012; 6 inches of .010; 6 inches of .008. This is the basic leader of 102 inches and is designed for a 4X rating when the tippet is added. I generally start with a tippet length of 36 inches and make a few casts. With a No. 12 fly the leader length will probably be about right. With smaller flies the tippet may have to be chopped to about 20 inches.

There are many different combinations I use for my own fly fishing. I have even experimented with leaders that go to extreme lengths of over 20 feet for fishing smooth flowing waters like Fall River or Hot Creek. Handling even a perfectly designed leader of this length is hard work. I only use them when it is absolutely essential. I have a buddy who says if you can get 10 feet of clean drift from a fly you can catch any trout that lives. This is true enough but I'll settle for dumb trout and hope for half this much drift.

Fly Reel

I consider the fly reel merely a place to store the line when not in use. To me the idea of the fly reel as something that can "balance" the rod is foolish. This is an old idea that doesn't make sense. The reel should be as light as possible. What tires your arm and causes you to lose your casting timing is the fact you are holding your arm in an unnatural position and fighting the weight of the rod and reel as well as the force of the line against the air. Anything you can do to lighten the weight will automatically improve your performance.

Wading Equipment

The key to fishing the white pocket water of riffles and small pools is the wading techniques used by the fisherman. I have tried just about every kind of equipment ever designed to assist the fisherman to do a better job of wading. For years I used felt-soled wading shoes as the best thing to allow the surest footing possible while wading slippery rocks. They are very effective, but they have become so hard to find, and they wear out so fast, I've changed to carpet sole waders.

Carpet Soles

Ted Fay, a very fine Dunsmuir fisherman, showed me how to profit from modern technology. To convert a regular pair of hip boots or chest waders for California stream fishing a piece of indoor-outdoor carpeting is cut to the shape of the soles of the boots. A liberal amount of contact cement is applied to both the boot and the carpeting and allowed to dry until it is tacky. This is moistened slightly with some more cement and the shaped carpet is placed carefully against the sole and heel of the boot foot. If the carpeting begins to slip or bulge out (as it will do with rounded soles found on most waders) wrap line around the boot tightly to make the contact total. Dry in the sun.

Fitted with these carpet soles, a wader or boot is about as non-slip as it is possible to get. The carpet is very durable. I can usually get an entire season of use from a single application, and I fish far more than most anglers. It is important to take care in applying the carpet. Try to weld the edges very securely with the contact cement. If a gap is left, the carpet will come loose as sand and small rocks get between the sole and the carpet. At any rate changing soles is cheap.

Wading Staff

A wading staff is a critical addition to a stream fisherman's equipment. In fishing most streams it is important to get to sections of stream other anglers cannot reach because they do not wade. A good wading staff can be used to assist a fisherman in wading currents where they flow strongest.

There are regular wading staffs on the market. Most come with a hook on the bottom. This hook is effective for pulling streamside brush down so you can retrieve a lure or fly. It's also handy for hooking something on shore to assist yourself out of the water.

I make my own wading staffs from fiberglass ski poles. The basket at the bottom of the pole is removed. Usually there is a hole through the bottom end of the pole used to secure the basket. This can be enlarged slightly by drilling and a large nail can be forced through the pole just above the metal tip. The nail is bent down pointing toward the handle to form a hook. The end is rounded off so no sharp point will snag wading gear.

The best length of a wading staff can be determined by each angler. The staff should reach from your arm extended straight out from the body, to the ground. This isn't critical, however. Any length pole will do, but any longer than this and they become hard to handle.

If you don't have a ski pole use a section of limb as a wading staff. You can then reach areas other anglers can never fish.

Add a length of strong twine, or shoe lace, tied to the handle in a loop. The loop should be large enough so you can slip it around your neck and under your off-casting arm. The loop is the proper length if the staff handle rides just behind the armpit about half way to the elbow when trailing in the current. In this position the staff is convenient and you can grab it if you should start to stumble in the current.

Trolling Equipment

The first troll I make is usually down the length of the lake a short distance out from the bank. I don't add any weight to the lure on the first pass unless I know the trout are not in shallow water or near shore. After a couple of passes inshore, I move out from shore into deeper water. Then at this point, I begin to add weight.

Light Line Trolling

I rig with very light lines on a standard 300 reel with either 4 lb. or even 2 lb. test monofilament. This size line has very little water resistance and it doesn't take very much weight to get relatively deep.

I rig this extra light line with a swivel about 4 ft. up the line from the lure. To this swivel I tie a dropper strand of about 2 ft. in length and I tie a very large snap swivel to the end of this dropper strand. The reason for this large snap swivel is so I can add a number of weights until I get down to the proper depth where the trout are holding. I've found that if I merely tie on a weight I am reluctant to change weights and weight combinations often, but with a simple snap swivel it is very easy to change weights while you are trying to dope out the best com-bination for a particular day of trolling.

The fact that there is so little re-sistance to the water with this very light line is the important factor in-volved in light line trolling. An ounce or two of lead will get a lure or bait down about as deep as is ever needed to take trout. Of course, when the trout are down more than 50 feet it is almost essential that the troller use the heavier gear and the extra heavy weights needed for probing these great depths.

A boat will give the angler access to the best fishing in the lakes and reservoirs covered in this guide.

Deep Trolling

For very deep trolling (up to 50 to 60 ft.) it is almost essential that the angler use heavy tackle. For my own deep trolling, which I seldom do because I do not like to fish with very heavy tackle even for the larger trout, I use an ocean salmon trolling outfit. This is a stiff boat rod of 6 or 7 ft. fitted with 20 to 30 lb. test monofilament and rigged with a sinker release.

A sinker release is a metal tube with a spring inside that allows the weight to fall free once a larger fish hits the lure or bait. These sinker releases allow the trout to fight as much as possible because they do not have to fight the heavy weight that is involved in this kind of trolling. But more important, the trout will often tear loose from the hooks if the heavy weight is still on the line after they are hooked.

You can buy weights called 'Cannonballs' by ocean salmon trollers, but these are comparatively expensive. I use a variety of beer cans and other cans filled with cement to get the same job done. You merely put a wire upright in the can and then fill it with concrete or cement. The wire is then bent into a loop and this is attached to the sinker release. The can is then cut away from the concrete weight if it doesn't shrink enough to pull free.

Accessories

Thermometers

In my own trout fishing, either in lakes or streams, I always find a fishing thermometer invaluable. If you can locate water that is no warmer than 60 degrees, and preferably 3 to 5 degrees cooler than that, you will have little trouble taking trout. Even in very cold spring-fed waters a thermometer will help you locate water of just the right temperature, and that's where the trout will be. Just a couple of degrees in temperature will alter trout behavior a great deal. Often, for example, where there are seeps from cold springs along the course of a stream, the trout will congregate in these areas in great numbers. It would be impossible to detect this temperature change merely by putting your hand in the water, but a thermometer will find such cold spots for you.

When I'm fishing a stream I hang a thermometer on a stringer, attach it to my waders, and allow it to drag in the current. This way I have a continual temperature check. By merely lifting the thermometer from the water periodically, I can locate prime areas that I might not necessarily notice as I am busy wading and fishing.

Electronic Locators

In my lake fishing, I use a Lowrance Fish Lokator. I realize the average angler doesn't have a chance to use one of these expensive electronic devices, but you shouldn't pooh-pooh these machines. By using one, I have learned some things about lake fishing that the majority of fishermen could never know. Also, what most anglers do not understand about these electronic machines is that they are far more useful and effective for locating bottom structure in a lake than they are for locating fish, for in a clear-water lake, any trout that is less than 30 or 40

An electronic locating device like this Lowrance Fish Lokator is very effective in checking out the bottom structure of lakes. Finding the underwater ridges is the key to taking trout of larger sizes. The Lokator is perfect for finding these.

feet deep will dart out from under the boat as it passes over and will never show up on the scope of the locator.

Polaroid Glasses

Polarized glasses, which cut surface glare, are a great help, particularly when fishing clear-water streams and lakes. With the aid of these glasses, you can see through the water perhaps 20 or 30 percent better than you can without them. You can spot deep holes and underwater obstructions much better while stream fishing, which can be a big advantage. And in lake fishing, it is often possible to climb a nearby hill or mountain and look down through the water to spot under-water structure. Trout generally like areas with clean bottoms so it is an advantage to know where under-water outcroppings of any kind are located. This is particularly true for bait fishermen. A bait fisherman wants to locate areas close to shore where the water is deep. He doesn't want to fish in an area that looks deep but is not because of a pro-truding underwater ledge.

Binoculars

I use a pair of binoculars a great deal when I am surveying a new stream. Often the roads along the banks run along the high side of the canyon where the stream flows. With glasses it is often possible, from the road, to spot sections of ideal water that probably never get fished much from the road. In a situation like this it is often worth the trouble and effort to scale the mountain to get at the water. It would be futile to scale down a steep mountain if you didn't know what kind of water was available. The fact a section is difficult to get to doesn't guarantee fishing will be good.

Beating Nets

In checking out the insect life for dry flies along streams like the Sacramento River, I generally use a short-handled, strong beating net. The idea here is to use the net to collect samples of the type of insects that are hiding during the daytime in the brush along the shorelines. This is done by beating the brush with a suitable net.

Maps

An angler should always try to get a good map of each new river or creek he is going to fish.

Forest Service Maps

The most common maps are those put out by the Forest Service. These are usually issued free at the ranger stations in the field and at the forest headquarters office for the National Forest in the area. They are fine detailed maps that can save an angler a lot of time and indicate possible points where stream access is possible.

Ownership Information

One important indication on the newer versions of these Forest Service maps is public land ownership in each forest. This is such an important facet it almost makes getting Forest Service maps mandatory. Areas in public domain are indicated in green. These are rarely 100 percent accurate because the Forest Service is continually buying and swapping for new lands. But the maps are, in general, accurate indications of where you may fish and where private property is located.

Geological Survey Maps

If I am planning an extensive amount of fishing in a given drainage I also like to have a set of Geological Survey maps of the area. These maps are the basic maps used by all agencies and they are extremely detailed. Every topographical feature, spring and minor stream is indicated. Often these can be used to locate streams, lakes and spots where fishing can be excellent in out-of-the-way spots.

I remember one spot near Coldstream Creek off Highway 89 in the High Sierra that showed up on the Geological Survey map as a bog. When I checked this spot out (it was about a mile from the road on an abandoned lumber road) I found a huge beaver pond complete with beaver. I took some of the finest browns and rainbows I've ever seen from this beaver lake. The stream that fed it was relatively small. It dried up altogether about a half mile downstream from the beaver dam, where it ran through a sandy rocky area. If you make a minute survey of Geological Survey maps you can find these off-beat spots while studying the area before you ever make the trip.

Bureau of Land Management Maps

Some of the streams and lakes worth fishing are on Bureau of Land Management lands. This agency does not put out good maps the fisherman can use. They do offer maps that show public ownership in the areas they control. These areas are extensive.

Park Service Maps

The Federal and State Park services usually have maps to offer the public. These are good as general indicators of what is available but normally you have to combine them with Geological Survey maps to be effective. Park services are more concerned with indicating what is available overall in their park, rather than in servicing the fisherman alone.

Addresses

Bureau of Land Management (BLM), 2800 Cottage Way, Sacramento, Ca. 95825.

U.S. Forest Service, 630 Sansome Street, San Francisco, Ca. 94100.

U.S. Geological Survey, 345 Middlefield Road, Menlo Park, Ca. 94025.

Using Guide Maps

The sketch maps included in *California Trout* are drawn specifically to assist the fisherman in getting to the actual fishing locations. These maps are not intended for any other purpose other than to aid the fisherman in getting to the water without a lot of extra time spent on discovery trips down many rough roads.

In the case of some of the streams and lakes the road and access systems are well established

and in other areas the road systems are in a continual state of change. Along the Sacramento River, for instance, the road systems have been established for many years and access problems are relatively stable from year to year. But on the McCloud River we face a situation where continual lumbering operations will even change the access picture from month to month.

At Davis Lake there has been an extensive amount of road and trail building and this lake may see more changes in the future. At Eagle Lake the roads and access trails are well established, although lumbering and other activities can open up or close down any of the roads other than county or state roads.

Map Symbols

In marking the maps with symbols we have attempted to simplify as much as possible. If a feature is not of great significance to the fisherman it is ignored on these maps. The location of camping areas is included because we found that many camp sites were not actually put on Forest Service and other government maps. We have found that fishermen will, and often prefer to, camp in unimproved spots where camping is allowed. The types of water available to the fisherman is denoted in detail in the text.

Where springs are noted it is because these spots have significance to the fisherman. Either they provide cold water areas at a lake or they significantly change the flow of a river.

The location of springs for drinking purposes or other reasons have been left off these maps. For this kind of information the U.S.

Geological Survey Quadrangle maps are far better to use.

The mileages involved in these maps are accurate but in some cases the river and the road systems have been exaggerated in order to clarify points of interest to the fisherman.

The maps have been left open enough so that the fisherman is able to make any personal marks on them with relative ease. The more intimate the fisherman becomes with each stream or lake the more effective he is when actually fishing.

The maps in this guide can be of great assistance because the fisherman can spend his time actually fishing rather than searching out routes to the water.

Trout Feed

The key to taking California trout is offering them something that comes close to imitating the food they normally eat. This may seem simple but it can have a direct bearing on consistent success. California waters are harder fished than most waters of the West and anglers who want to be consistently successful are well-advised to spend some time and effort studying the diet of trout in any given stream system or lake.

There have been drastic changes in the biotope of our mountain waters due to so much damming. There has been a great deal of manipulation of bait species in the past 100 years. Some of the introductions of new types of baitfish and competing species have been very haphazard. Fish & Game Department management was relatively unsophisticated in the last century and a lot of mistakes were made. Some fisheries, such as the Lahontan Basin trout fishery, which once produced remarkable cutthroat trout fishing, had introductions of other species that literally eliminated the original trout.

Imitate What Is There

The modern trout fisherman should try to imitate the species of fish and insect life that remain in any given drainage. This is not an impossible task. Although there are thousands of different species of aquatic insects and hundreds of types of baitfish, there are only a few species worth notice from the angler's point of view. A general outline of these will eliminate the bulk of these species.

Baitfish

The most logical way for the serious lure fisherman to go about his trout fishing is to take it for granted that about the only thing he can reasonably imitate is a small baitfish. I have made extensive experiments with plastic lures formed to imitate aquatic insects with little success. They will take trout but the fish seem to want only a suggestion of insect life, much better done with flies than almost identical molded duplications.

The easiest way to select a baitfish to imitate is to assume that the young of the species you are fishing for are on hand in large numbers. In every stream or lake you can assume that if rainbow, brown or brook trout are there to be taken, there will be a large supply of the fry and young of these species. In many cases you can confirm this by merely looking in the shallow sections of lakes and in protected backwaters of most streams. Almost any

wobbler or spoon of the right size will do the job of imitating these colorful young trout. Many smaller plugs also imitate these small trout very closely. The only problem then becomes delivering the lure in a lifelike way.

Most anglers fish lures far too fast. A young trout or baitfish does not swim fast and it does not move through the water at a steady pace. Instead, the secret of survival for a young fish is a matter of darting and dodging from faster predatory fish. They can never hope to outswim a larger fish; they survive by being able to maneuver better. A retrieve that is irregular is better than one that is steady.

Fish the Edges

Trout and other baitfish do not generally swim freely in the open waters of a lake or stream. They rarely venture far from some sort of cover. This is a matter of finding a secure habitat without violently flowing water where they can hide from predators. The edge of a piece of fast-flowing water is generally a more productive place to fish than the center of a large, deep hole. You will find much more baitfish action around the edges of a lake. Baitfish generally tend to hold right on the bottom where they find the feed necessary to sustain life and a place to hide in the rubble of the bottom.

It is usually better, therefore, to allow a lure to settle to the bottom, or very near the bottom of a lake or stream, before retrieving it. The combination of a slow, erratic and deep retrieve is normally best for all situations. On rare occasions you will find trout that prefer a fast-moving lure. This should be attempted if the slow retrieve doesn't produce.

Some California Baitfish

The California Fish and Game Department has published a brief rundown on baitfish species in "Freshwater Nongame Fishes of California." It provides an outline of the types of smaller fish trout are likely to find in California waters. Some of these, such as the threadfin shad has had a remarkable effect on trout fishing in lakes where it has been introduced. There is some indication the species can even be implanted into new waters by eggs attached to the feathers of birds. These "accidental" introductions may mean we will have this baitfish species in all our waters eventually, even in lakes they were never intended for.

The threadfin is a silvery fish with a yellowish-green to bluish-green back divided about half way up the length of the body. The fins are yellowish to yellow-green. Lures and flies should have these combinations of colors. The fish can range from string-like larvae about a half-inch long to adult fish several inches in length. They spawn when the water reaches about 70 degrees. Since the eggs need water temperature of about 80 degrees to hatch, few will be found at higher elevations.

Pond smelt are very silvery. They are found in the Yuba South Fork drainage. They were imported from Japan in 1959. They can be imitated by nearly any silver wobbling lure or a silver and white streamer or bucktail fly.

Suckers

Although suckers may compete with the smaller trout for food, they provide an excellent source of food for larger trout. In general the suckers are a dark but not mottled fish. There are several species in California and most trout waters have some form of the species. An imitation that will work anywhere is a streamer that is solid and dull with mixed gray and brown hair or feathers over an all-silver tinsel body. Lures like wobblers that are dull-colored work well.

Threadfin shad (Dorosoma petenense). Dorosoma: *lance body;* petenense: *Lake Peten, Yucatan.*

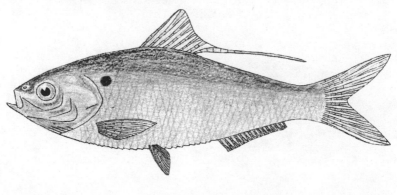

Hardhead

The hardhead minnow is found in all the Central Valley drainages. The adult looks a lot like a squawfish but the young are good trout food. They are bronze on the back and the belly shades to silver or cream. When young these minnows feed on insects; when adult on other fish and aquatic plants. This makes them direct competitors with trout for food

Squawfish

The squawfish also competes directly with trout. They grow to be two or three feet long. The young are usually dark on the back, shading to silver on the belly. They are imitated by nearly any lure or fly with flash. There is some orange in the fins. They are found in streams tributary to the Central Valley.

Redside

The Lahontan redside is an important baitfish for larger trout in the eastern drainages of the Sierra and in streams and lakes north of the American River. Its name comes from the distinctive red or pink stripe running the length of the minnow on the side. This shades to pink during most of the year, turning red when spawning season arrives. Lures and flies should have a reddish or dark stripe to imitate this baitfish successfully.

Pond smelt (Hypomesus olidus). Hypomesus: *below middle, referring to ventral fins;* olidus: *oily.*

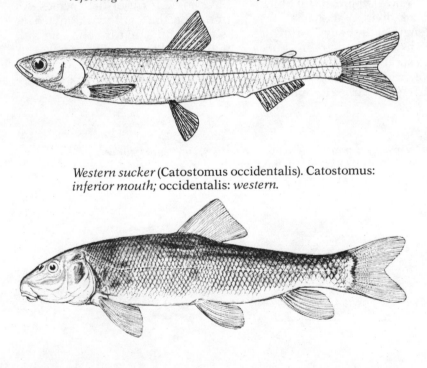

Western sucker (Catostomus occidentalis). Catostomus: *inferior mouth;* occidentalis: *western.*

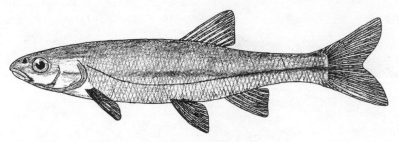

Hardhead (Mylopharodon cononcephalus). Mylopharodon: *throat tooth grinder;* conocephalus: *cone head.*

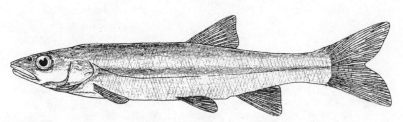

Sacramento squawfish (Ptychocheilus grandis). Ptychocheilus: *folded lip;* grandis: *large.*

Tui Chub

There are four different chub varieties in California waters. They are an important baitfish species in mountain waters. Though the larger tui chub is a thick fish the minnows are very streamlined. They run in color from olive green on the back to white and yellow combinations on the belly. They have been found with brassy-green and even silver-green on the back shading to silver on the belly. The best imitations are half dark above and white or lemon on the belly. They are not a fast-water fish and are found in lakes, particularly around grassy or rocky cover, and in deep pools in rivers.

Sculpin and Sticklebacks

There are several species of spiny baitfish in California waters. The sculpin and stickleback are not nearly as noticeable as other baitfish species because they inhabit riffles where they are difficult to detect. The best imitations of either species are mottled flies or lures. Only a few lakes have these species.

Baitfish Imitations

In my opinion, the vast majority of standard wet flies used today are taken by the trout as small baitfish. An angler should make some concession to color. Most of the minnows found in California waters are

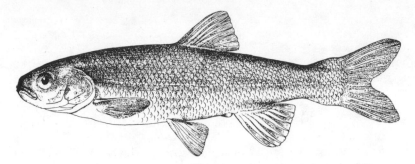

Lahontan redside (Richardsonius egregius). Richardsonius: *in honor of Sir John Richardson;* egregius: *surprising elegant.*

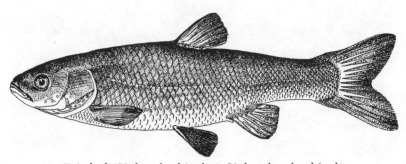

Tui chub (Siphateles bicolor). Siphateles: *far;* bicolor: *two-colored.*

lighter on the bottom than on the upper half of the body. A fly with a body of tinsel will make a minnow-like imitation. A bright-colored body material also gives a fly flash. Generally materials that soak up water, such as silk, are not too good because they change colors drastically when wet.

Size is probably more important than color in offering minnow imitations. If a trout follows a lure and then refuses it at the last minute, it is usually necessary to go to a smaller lure to get the fish to hit. Very rarely will a trout want a larger lure. Yet it happens often enough that an angler should have larger lures and flies available to offer them. I have found streamers and bucktails with an overlay of peacock hurl spears very effective. I think this is because the hurl gives just the right bronze and greenish flash to the fly. I've also found lures with some green in them effective. Red is accepted by most anglers as a primary color but I've found green to be more productive, except during spawning periods.

California Trout Diet

In California trout fishing the angler who fishes many streams and lakes will find an astounding variety of different aquatic and terrestrial insects. Because most California stream systems have their headwaters at very high altitude and flow down a vertical drop of about 10,000 feet, the angler is faced with the job of imitating insects of many kinds even in a single stream. The many reservoirs further complicate the problem of duplicating insects in trout diets. Some insects will live only in still waters of reservoirs. Other species live only in flowing water.

Observation

It should be obvious to any trout fisherman that if he is on a section of stream or a lake when a big hatch is coming off the water, he should try to duplicate the insect the trout are feeding on. It would be silly to use a dark pattern when a pale mayfly is coming off the water. More than color, however, the size of the fly is the critical element. Good observation of all factors influencing what the insect population is doing will pay off for the angler. These particulars are covered in detail in many books on trout fishing. In California waters the only difference is the multiplicity of insect populations due to the variations in altitudes and the types of water available.

If you are a student of insects there is a very good book on the subject, "Aquatic Insects of California," edited by Robert Usinger, Univers-

Riffle sculpin (Cottus gulosus). Cottus: *old European name;* gulosus: *greedy.*

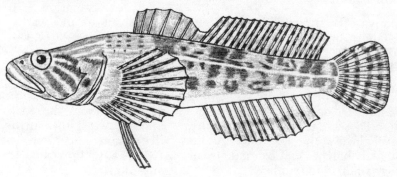

Threespine stickleback (Gasterosteus aculeatus). Gasterosteus: *belly bone;* aculeatus: *spined.*

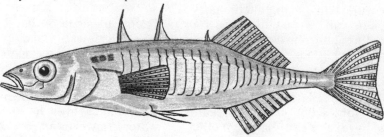

ity of California Press. This is a general guide to California underwater insects and is not limited to trout feeding habits. We'll deal here with only a few insects that it is possible for a fair fly tier to imitate easily.

Stoneflies

Most presentations on fishing with flies usually start with a discussion of mayflies. I feel the stonefly and caddis fly are more important in our waters. Nearly every stream system in the state has both stonefly and caddis flies. There *are* plenty of mayfly hatches in California but I want to point up the importance of the other two species in the diet of California trout.

Life History

Many of the stonefly hatches occur in late spring and early summer but some occur even during the winter. This makes stoneflies and their larvae a year-around item in the trout diet. Some of the hatches, called "salmon fly" hatches, can be spectacular. These large flies only occur in a few places. The less spectacular stonefly hatches can be made up of very small individuals.

The female generally lays her eggs much as mayflies do, by flying along and dipping her abdomen on the water while in flight. This can be spectacular because of the size of the flies and because stoneflies are notoriously poor flyers. When the larger females begin laying their eggs, they often hit the water with an audible splatting noise. This is important when fishing streams that have hatches of large stoneflies. You can often create a hatch of your own by splatting large flies on the water, even if there have been no significant hatches for a long time on that particular stream. Trout tend to ignore any fly that isn't splatted on the water when they are feeding on an actual hatch.

Stonefly Nymphs

The nymph stage of the stonefly is the most important to the angler. It is very likely that popular flies like the Wooly Worm are taken by trout because they do a passable job of imitating the larger stonefly nymphs. The actual nymph is not free-swimming and to imitate them correctly a fly should be fished deep and slow.

When the stonefly is ready to mate it crawls up on rocks or stems of water vegetation. It rests a distance out of the water until the adult emerges. After waiting to dry the adult flies to streamside brush. Some nymphs undoubtedly get washed away in the current where trout can take them without plucking them from the rocks as they climb toward the surface. A free drift, slow and deep with a few twitches, will properly imitate this situation.

Caddis Flies and Sedges

Caddis flies are on hand in nearly every fresh water lake or stream in California. The American sedges, a form of caddis, are the flies you see swarming near almost every trout stream during the warm months. They "dance" over the surface of the water in swarms and are often thick in streamside vegetation.

Life History

The female caddis deposits her eggs in or near the water, usually by crawling underwater. The larva form is the all-important case worm so familiar to most fishermen. The larvae build their tubes from bits of stream or lake bottom material, using bits of wood, leaves and stones which they cement together to form the protective covering they need. These tubes can be plucked off stones in quiet backwaters of streams and used for bait. They can be fished case and all or the larva can be taken out of the case. If you check the stomach contents of trout you'll often find bits of stone and wood. This comes from eating caddis worms, case and all.

Most of the life of the caddis larvae is spent in contact with the bottom. To imitate them properly a fly should be fished slow and deep. A majority of caddis flies I've checked have gold or cream bodies, with heads and legs of dark brown or black. A good fly can be tied to represent these larvae with very sparse and dark hackle. The proper size can be found by merely pulling a few caddis cases from the rocks and checking the size of the actual larvae. The combination of the right color and size will nearly always give a good measure of success. Though I doubt trout see caddis larvae out of their cases too often, they will hit flies of the right size that represent the worm inside the case. I've experimented with flies tied to indicate the caddis case, which I've fished by rolling along the bottom, but with poor results.

A fly tied with a few feathers flat across the back of the fly will yield some good trout if it is fished in the surface film of the water. Though adult caddis are not nearly as important as the larvae in trout diet, they often fall to the water, and dead females are washed downstream. Trout recognize them and flies that imitate them. The adult caddis can be identified when at rest by the wings folded like a tent over the body. The adult stonefly, in contrast, lays its wings flat across the top of the body.

Mayflies

Most of the angling lore in the U.S. devoted to mayflies and trout has little application to California trout fishing. In none of the eastern, midwestern and Rocky Mountain states

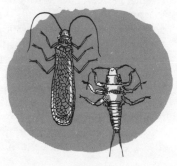

Stonefly and nymph

Caddis worm in its case and the caddis fly

will you find stream systems that vary so much in altitude in such short lengths of stream. The descent from around 10,000 feet to sea level in such a short distance makes the mayfly traditions of the West Coast far more complex than is characteristic in most other streams.

Different Stream Types

The typical California stream is rough flowing in comparison to those in most of the rest of the country. We have only a few high plateau rivers, like the Owens, where the flow of waer is smooth and relatively even over a long stretch. A typical California river will roar through a steep canyon and plunge down several feet for every mile of flow. There are more sections of white, riffle water per mile in California waters than in streams in most states. This difference in water type calls for different mayfly fishing techniques.

Life History

The life history of the mayfly is worth noting briefly. Eggs are usually laid while the female is in flight. She dips her tail on the water repeatedly, washing a few eggs off each time. The eggs become nymphs during the ensuing months. When ready to become an adult these nymphs swim to the surface. In some species the nymph swims back and forth between the surface and the bottom several times. Eventually the nymph floats on the surface. The nymph's back splits and the first version of the adult, known as the dun or subimago, usually rides the nymph skin until the wings and body dry.

The dun flies to streamside brush or rocks for about 24 hours. The skin again splits and the final stage of the adult emerges. The mayfly is the only insect that sheds its skin a second time. The sexually mature adult, called the imago, mates, lays eggs, and normally dies within a matter of hours. In most mayfly species the final adult stage is more colorful than the dun. The life of the female mayfly usually ends when she spends her energy and falls to the water as a spinner. The males exhaust themselves, often flying for miles above the stream, and are not as numerous as spinners on the water. When the mating dance ends, trout will swarm to the surface to feed on the female spinners that drop to the water.

Imitating Life Cycle

This very brief outline of the life cycle of the mayfly points up the fact there are many stages of the insect's life that have to be taken into consideration. The nymph form of the mayfly is far more important to trout (and therefore to fishermen) than the adult, winged version. Nymphs are on hand year-around as a source of food for trout. Like other aquatic insects, more than 90 percent of the mayflies that are eaten by the trout are nymphs, rather than the winged version. When there is no hatch with trout actively feeding, it is usually better to fish with nymph imitations rather than with floating patterns.

When trout are feeding on duns, the real "hatch" as far as fishermen are concerned, they usually ignore all other insects. It is critical to capture specimens of what the trout are feeding on and examine them, since it is important to fish each stage of the life cycle correctly, even in rough-flowing streams like ours.

Mayfly Nymph Fishing

Although matching the hatch and critical nymph fishing are essential in only a few California streams, there are hundreds, even thousands, of lakes where proper nymph fishing techniques are essential to consistent success. Although some mayfly nymphs crawl up rocks or reeds to reach the surface, most swim to the surface.

In many lakes an angler will see trout surfacing when there are no visible flies on the surface. If you watch closely you will see the head is not coming to the surface; only the tail swirls the surface. These trout are nymphing just under the surface and disturb the surface only when they turn, just under the surface, to intercept the swimming nymphs.

To fish a new hatch merely cast out, allow the nymph fly to sink (it need not go all the way to the bottom) and slowly retrieve. Few nymphs of the mayfly swim fast, so a slow retrieve is best. Most nymphs are drab or dull in color, particularly lake nymphs.

Dry Fly Fishing

In order to imitate a floating dun or a spent spinner an angler should attempt to capture a specimen. Size is particularly critical in mayfly imitations on the still water of lakes but can affect results even in the fast-moving sections of a stream. It is advisable to match the color closely if you can but, if you have to choose between matching color or size, the size of the fly you offer is most critical. You should use as long and as light a leader as you can for fly fishing in lakes and still sections of a stream. If, for instance, you can accurately cast 6X leaders of 14 to 20 feet you should use them. If you can only handle a short leader it is more important to deliver the fly lightly than to have a really long leader. In clear still water the leader alone will spook trout.

When dry fly fishing in the riffle or pocket water of our generally rough mountain streams, the main problem faced by California fishermen is to have a fly that will float at all. This is the reason you will see heavy hackled flies like a Bivisible or deer hair flies so much in use on our waters. Hollow hair flies like the Horner Deer Hair are made of material that has built-in floatabil-

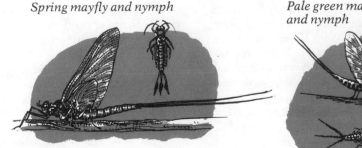

Spring mayfly and nymph

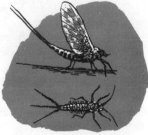

Pale green mayfly and nymph

Black dragon and nymph

Chromagrion damselfly and nymph

ity. The Bivisibles perform the dual function of being readily visible to an angler fishing whitewater edges and also being very floatable. Again, size is the important element. If the trout are not hitting, and you can't determine what they are feeding on, experiment with various size flies until you get a rise.

Dragonflies and Damselflies

The many conspicuous dragonflies and damselflies are a part of fishing anywhere in California. About the only time trout feed on the adult versions is right after a large number of these insects have hatched. At this early stage the adult fly is very flabby and a weak flier. If there is a considerable wind blowing off shore during this stage of the hatch, the soft adults will be blown onto the water. A large fly tied to imitate these can sometimes be effective in areas where husks of nymph skins are visible, attached to reeds or rocks in a lake or stream area. These flies are most effective if they are activated so they seem to be struggling a great deal on the surface.

Active Nymphs

In most waters the nymphs of the dragonflies and damselflies are excellent trout food. The dragonfly nymph is one of the most active and rapacious of all aquatic insects, actively pursuing and devouring other insects from the time it is first formed. This activity makes them more available to trout than many secretive insects that spend most of their lives under bottom cover. Probably one of the reasons the Wooly Worm fly is so effective in our waters is because this usually stubby, dark fly comes close to duplicating dragonfly nymphs. They are bottom dwellers and the majority of species frequent faster sections of a stream in and near riffles. They are not free swimmers, so a fly fished to imitate them should be fished slow and deep with a twitching retrieve.

Fishfly, Alderfly and Dobsonfly

Although fishflies, alderflies and dobsonflies are available to California trout in nearly all drainages, I have never opened a trout stomach and found any of the adults or larvae present. In California waters these insects are more commonly found in the lower elevations of most streams. Occasionally I have found fishing imitations of these insects valuable. In the case of a dobsonfly or alderfly it is often good to fish downstream from overhanging brush and bridges since these insects lay their eggs in streamside brush and the underside of bridges. Some of the adults undoubtedly fall or are blown into the water where trout feed on them.

Being unable to confirm how important these three flies are in the diet of California trout, I have taken a generalized approach to fishing imitations. I believe any fairly large nymph pattern will imitate dobsonfly nymphs. Smaller nymph pat-

terns in dark or somber colors will serve as imitations of the fishfly and alderfly.

Midge Fishing

Midge fishing can provide some very fine sport. There are literally hundreds of species of midge in our trout waters. You will often see midges swarming over the water, generally in the evenings from spring through fall. Some species scoot across the water. I think the reason tiny fly patterns like the Adams and Cahills, tied on hooks No. 18 through No. 22, are so effective is that these patterns come pretty close to imitating many of our midges.

Blue darner dragonfly and nymph

Fishfly and larva

Dobsonfly and larva (hellgrammite)

Alderfly and larva (hellgrammite)

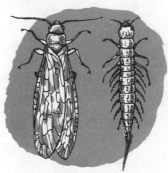

Life History

Midges begin to be important trout food when they are in the larval stage. Most species of California midges form small tubcs of bottom material where they hide during the hours of daylight. In the evening they become active and most move out of the tubes to feed. They are usually round and not too hairy. A simple imitation can be made by tying a short piece of rubber to a tiny hook. Most larvae at this stage are under a half-inch in length, so imitations of this stage should be small. Different-colored pieces of rubber —red, white and yellow, in that order of importance—with tying thread around them can be used to make an accurate duplicate. Naturally they should be fished slow and deep. If the rubber is tied to the hook only in the center the imitation will undulate in the water as it is moved slowly.

Midge Pupae

Every trout fisherman has run into times when trout are feeding on something seemingly invisible and refuse to hit anything offered to them. In California this usually means trout are feeding on a hatch of midges. The pupal and early adult stages are very important to trout fishermen. After going into the pupal stage in the tube used by the larva, the emerging pupa rises and hangs suspended from the surface film of the water. Pupae must breathe air or die. I have seen lakeshores with windrows of discarded larval cases from midge hatches and there are times when the entire surface of the lake or stream seems covered with emerging pupae.

If you look closely you will see the pupa resembles a worm from a quarter-inch to just over a half-inch in length. If you irritate the pupa it will wriggle its wormlike body and often go under the water, only to return quickly to the surface. This is what happens if there is a fair wind blowing when the pupae hatch is on. The insects, in this stage, are readily available to trout, which gorge on them. For this reason a tailless fly is usually more effective than one of the common mayfly imitations. These flies can be fished effectively on the surface or just below the surface. Size is more important than color for a successful imitation. The primary colors for California nymphs are tan, yellow, gray, black, white, brown and green, in that order.

Adult Midge

It is the early adult stage of the midge that usually causes so much activity among trout. The adult pulls itself from the pupa and sits on the surface. With many species there is a great deal of commotion at this stage as the adults flounder on the water and skim about. This activity makes them very noticeable to trout. The imitation of the adult is not nearly as critical as the larval or pupal stage except in size. Most adults are about a half-inch long; in many cases they are only half this large, especially at higher elevations. You can use a lightly hackled dry fly of nearly any kind to imitate the adult stage of the midge. Probably a selection of tiny Bivisible dry flies will do about as good a job as any. This pattern can be skittered along the surface and jiggled without making it sink. Most midge pat-

Midge and larva

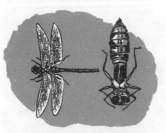

Green darner and nymph

Water scavenger beetle and larva

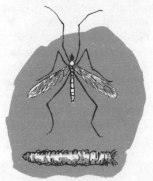

Crane fly and larva

terns I use are tied on hooks size No. 16 through No. 22.

Craneflies

If there are craneflies in an area where you are fishing there will be no doubt about it. These are the big mosquito-like flies you see bumbling about streams and lakes. Some species live in the water in a larval form that is just an enlarged version of the midge larva. The larva can be from a quarter-inch to as much as two inches in length. The pupa stage is usually passed in boggy ground above water. The adult emerges and you can see swarms of males during the mating flights. The female deposits her eggs on the water much like a mayfly adult. About the only way you can imitate the adults is with a large hackle fly tied on a small hook. I suspect many times trout are hitting commercially tied flies, which usually have too much hackle, thinking they are crane fly imitations.

Beetles and Ants

At certain times of the year terrestrial beetles form an important part of trout diet. I have opened many trout stomachs during the summer months and found them stuffed with beetles. This is particularly true of brush streams where there are literally millions of beetles of different types in the streamside foliage. Evidently what happens is that at certain times huge numbers of beetles get active and some of them are pushed or find their way into the water. It would be impossible to tie flies to imitate every form of beetle that might find its way into a lake or stream. I merely have several patterns tied in the Jassid fashion and in several sizes for those times when beetles are in the trout diet.

I have never found an ant in a trout stomach, not even when flying ants and termites are active. However, flies tied in ant form will take trout. I feel a Black Gnat pattern in several sizes does an adequate job of imitating ants.

Terrestrial Insects

It is safe to say every form of terrestrial insect in a given area eventually gets into the trout diet at one time or another. Flies like the Muddler Minnow are probably effective because they imitate grasshoppers or some other form of large terrestrial insect. Naturally, if the angler sees a meadow full of 'hoppers near a lake or stream, it can be assumed trout will readily take a fly tied to imitate these insects. Moths, bees and other insects often swarm near trout water. If the angler sees these insects on or near the water, flies that resemble them in size and color are usually effective.

Trout Flies

Probably every fly ever tied to take trout anywhere has been used successfully in California waters at one time or another. Through the years I've found some patterns that have been more consistently successful than others. The most important thing is to have a variety of different types of flies, and a wide selection of fly sizes to offer trout. The selection listed here is not meant to be complete. Rather, I am attempting to point out the various types of flies that are preferred by California trout. Each fly selected is representative of a collection of similiar flies.

Wooly Worm

The Wooly Worm pattern is a gray hackle over a peacock hurl body. In my immediate collection I also have Wooly Worm flies tied with chenille, wool and sack bodies in many colors. These flies should also be weighted in some ties for those times it is necessary to get deep in fast-flowing water. I like to have this key pattern in sizes No. 6 through No. 20 or No. 22. If an angler doesn't tie his own flies, and if his budget is limited, the Wooly Worm should be the first wet fly added to the collection. It is more important to trout fishing success to have a single pattern like the Wooly Worm in as many sizes and colors as possible than to have many different kinds of patterns.

Muskrat Nymph

The Muskrat Nymph is illustrative of a simple-to-tie type of nymph imitation. This particular fly is tied with an animal fur body and a head of peacock hurl. This type of fly does an adequate job of imitating many different types of aquatic insects. I also have flies of this type tied with other types and colors of body-tying material and with hackles of many different substances. It is the type

and size of the flies that is important. I generally use them in sizes No. 8 through No. 20.

Green Nymph

This particular fly has been very effective for me. The body is green wool, hackle and tail gray hackle fibres, and wings of short sections of peacock hurl. This fly (and others in different colors, sizes and composition) is a good one to try if there isn't some immediate indication of a hatch. It's what I call a searching pattern for those times when trout aren't actively feeding. You can gather together almost any fly tied in the common wet fly manner into this same group type. I don't know what these flies suggest to trout.

Black Gnat

The Black Gnat wet is another key pattern for California trout. Like the Wooly Worm, this pattern will take trout from all of our trout waters. Note how the fly is tied sparse. This is something I insist on whether the fly is meant to be fished wet or dry. Most commercially tied flies,

Wooly Worm

Muskrat Nymph

Green Nymph   *Black Gnat (wet)*

both wet and dry, are tied with too much hackle. Again, if the angler is strapped for money, he'd be better off to concentrate on getting flies of this single pattern in sizes from No. 6 through No. 22. The body on this tie is black wool, hackle and tail are black hackle and wings black hackle tips.

Stonefly Nymph

The Stonefly Nymph is another fly selected to illustrate a type of fly rather than an individual fly. In this particular pattern the body is brown floss on the rear half and brown wool on the front half. There is no hackle around the head of the fly. Instead, hackle fibres are tied on at the rear of the thorax and then tied down facing past the eye of the hook. In this particular fly the hackle fibres are brown. The fibres are divided to imitate feelers common to many aquatic insects. The tail is sparse and divided to imitate the tails found on many aquatic insects. It is the basic shape that is important in this type of fly. I usually weight these patterns. An angler who ties his own flies can let his im-

agination go when tying this type of sinking fly. If he compares this type of tie with aquatic insects collected from the waters where he fishes, he can make far better imitations than he can buy in most stores. I vary the size of these flies as much as possible. I've found sizes No. 8 through No. 16 the most successful.

Gray Hackle

This is a standard Gray Hackle Yellow. This fly illustrates the common ties found on most commercial flies. The body is yellow floss. The over-wrap is black fly tying thread wrapped down and back to present a segmented effect to the body. This, by the way, can be done on any fly pattern. It has the effect of giving a pleasantly segmented look to the fly, such as that found in most aquatic insects, and it makes the body much stronger. The wing and tail are mallard breast feathers.

In my own opinion nearly any wet fly can be tied with or without a tail, except perhaps in the case where you are trying to duplicate some important form of underwater insect, such as stonefly nymphs.

Gray Hackle (wet)

Stonefly Nymph

In my own fly book I use the tail mainly to indicate which flies have been weighted with fuse lead wire and which have not. When actually on the water it is difficult to determine if an individual fly is weighted or not. In my fly box the flies with tails are weighted. Those without tails are not weighted.

Brindle Nymph

The Brindle Nymph was tied specifically to imitate a nymph I found in several high Sierra streams. The body is black wool. The wing pads are brown to gray animal hair. Hackle, only on the bottom, is light brown. Along the back is brindle chenille tied flat. The tail is turkey fibres. This is a good illustration of an effective tie you can make if you do some collecting of insects in a specific area. The insects were all the same and a No. 10 hook fit them exactly. I have taken trout with this fly in many areas, even though I couldn't find the actual insect in the water. I feel this type of fly represents a general buggy tie that is effective on trout nearly everywhere.

The idea is to represent aquatic insects in general when you are fishing blind. Naturally, if you discover specific insects in a given body of water, an attempt should be made to duplicate these insects as closely as possible.

Dark Caddis

The Dark Caddis is tied the same way as the Muskrat Caddis except that tiny hackle tip wings have been added. This shows the possible variations on a single pattern. Often I've found even minute changes in basic patterns will make them more productive. When I get a winning combination like the Muskrat Caddis I experiment with variations in the way I tie them until I arrive at an effective pattern. With this method you can work with a pattern until you get it nearly perfect. The main problem in my own fishing is that I keep on the move and do not fish the same waters year after year. If you fish the same lakes and streams each year it is doubly important that you work with patterns imitating insects in those waters.

Brown Razorback

The tie for the Brown Razorback is identical to the Brindle Razorback except the body is brown wool and the chenille is black. This is another case where an attempt was made to duplicate an insect directly. This fly was eagerly accepted by trout in the South Fork of the Pit River and has also taken trout in many other streams.

Nymph Patterns

I have literally hundreds of patterns in my fly box and it would be impossible to list all the different types

I've ever used for California trout fishing. Instead I'll concentrate on the ones I've found take more and larger trout. I do the bulk of my own fishing with sinking flies. I consider the reason they are productive is that trout get at least 90 percent of their food from underwater insects and other types of underwater food. The pictures illustrate some of the better patterns for California trout from my own fly box.

Insect Flies

Black Nymph: *Body:* black chenille or wool. *Tail:* brown, gray or black hackle. *Ribbing:* gold or silver oval

Black Gnat

Brindle Nymph

Dark Caddis

Brown Razorback

tinsel. *Hackle:* black, trimmed so only the sides protrude.

The general idea behind this type of fly is to provide an imitation of a wide range of the insects found in our trout waters. I use this pattern when the Wooly Worm pattern is rejected. Often trout will refuse the Wooly Worm in bright water simply because it has so many fibres on it. You can make an effective substitute for this pattern by merely trimming most of the hackle from a Wooly Worm.

Blue Nymph: *Body:* blue chenille or wool. *Tail:* teal or mallard flank. *Ribbing:* silver or gold tinsel. *Hackle:* flank feather spears.

This fly is effective in many waters in California. It is generally buggy. The hackle can be tied either at the side to represent legs or toward the front to represent feelers.

Brown Nymph: *Body:* brown or gold wool topped with alternate winds of white chenille. *Tail:* brown hackle. *Ribbing:* black tying thread wound down and back. *Hackle:* black, below only.

The object with this fly is to imitate the common caddis larva out of its case. This fly, and others like it, are extremely effective in nearly all California trout waters. The object is to give a golden or luminescent appearance to the body. Sometimes it helps to collect a sample from a specific body of water. In some areas the caddis larva has brown legs rather than black. Size is critical.

Black Bug: *Body:* black chenille, wool or peacock hurl. *Hackle:* coat trimmed only on sides front and back.

This simple-to-tie fly is very effective. It is another offshoot of the Wooly Worm pattern used when trout are fussy.

Caddis Worm: *Body:* gray or brindle chenille or wool. *Hackle:* peacock hurl fibres. *Tail:* peacock hurl fibres.

Often the caddis found in dark or discolored waters is subdued in color. This larva imitation is more effective than the regular caddis tie in these cases. Again, it is important to collect samples of what is available for the trout to feed on and to attempt to imitate what is there.

Shrimp: *Body:* red or fluorescent wool. *Ribbing:* silver or gold tinsel. *Hackle:* orange or red, palmered and trimmed along the top. *Wing:* red or orange fur tied down at rear of fly to form a rough shrimp shape.

Some waters in California have fresh water shrimp, or scuds. Some scuds are tiny and accurate size is more important in this imitation than anything else. I tie mine on hooks from No. 6 through No. 20.

Gold Back: *Body rear:* gold tinsel, *front:* black wool. *Wing:* peacock hurl. *Tail:* peacock hurl.

This is another attempt to imitate caddis larvae. In fairly roiled water the flash of the gold section helps trout to locate this tie. It has proved a good pattern in nearly all California waters.

Gray Bug: *Body:* gray animal fur or wool. *Ribbing:* black tying thread. *Hackle:* gray. *Wings:* gray hackle tips. *Tail:* gray hackle tip.

This fly — and others tied like it with short wings of black, brown or other dark shades — is tied to represent many kinds of mayfly nymphs. The wing sac on a mayfly nymph is nearly black just before the nymph is ready to hatch. It is important to indicate the general color and outline of the mayfly nymph imitation. I usually strengthen this tie with an overwrap of black tying thread to give the body a segmented look.

Gray Nymph: *Body:* spun animal fur. *Ribbing:* gold tinsel. *Hackle:* duck flank segments. *Tail:* duck flank.

This fly is another takeoff on the Gray Bug pattern.

Olive Nymph: *Body:* olive wool. *Ribbing:* black tying thread. *Hackle:* teal flank tied as feelers on sides only. *Tail:* teal flank.

Red Nymph: *Body:* red wool, rear, peacock hurl front. *Ribbing:* black tying thread. *Hackle and Tail:* guinea feelers.

Rust Nymph: *Body:* yellow or gold wool. *Ribbing:* brown wool. *Hackle:* guinea. *Tail:* guinea.

Yellow and Brown: *Body:* yellow or gold wool, brown chenille tied along back. *Ribbing:* black tying thread. *Hackle:* Brown hackle fibres on bottom only. *Tail:* black hackle fibres.

These last three patterns are general flies I've found effective in most California trout waters. Probably the last two represent caddis larvae. The Red Nymph is a fairly gaudy pattern that trout accept in most waters, it probably imitates a shrimp or scud fairly closely.

Streamers

The streamers I use in California waters are not really new patterns. In general, a streamer is used to represent smaller fish that trout feed on. Almost all baitfish are light on the stomach and darker on the back. I have found that streamers tied with barred wings are usually effective no matter where they are fished. I could probably do well with any one of the patterns I normally carry as long as there were several sizes. In streamer fishing size is not nearly as critical as it is in fishing insect imitations. Smaller fish, naturally, come in many sizes. But if you see a trout refuse to hit a fly after following, usually changing to a smaller pattern will bring success.

Of particular note are streamers made with marabou wings or an overlay of peacock hurl. These two materials are very effective no matter where you fish. Too, any streamer pattern seems to attract generally larger fish than are taken on other types of flies. All trout become cannibalistic when they grow older. This is another good reason to use streamers.

Black Marabou: *Body:* black chenille. *Ribbing:* fluorescent red wool. *Tag:* fluorescent red wool, wide. *Hackle:* orange, under only. *Wing:* black marabou thinly tied.

Blue Devil: *Body:* gold tinsel. *Tail:* golden pheasant. *Hackle:* gray with golden pheasant under. *Wing:* gray hackle feather, jungle cock.

Gold: *Body:* gold tinsel. *Tail:* golden pheasant. *Hackle:* red. *Wing:* white bucktail under brown.

Gray Ghost: *Body:* orange wool. *Ribbing:* silver tinsel. *Hackle:* peacock hurl, under only, long with white bucktail. *Wing:* gray hackle feathers, golden pheasant cheek, jungle cock eye.

Jersey Minnow: *Body:* gold tinsel. *Tail:* golden pheasant. *Hackle:* brown and pink, mixed. *Wing:* badger hackle feathers.

Needabeh: *Body:* red wool. *Ribbing:* silver tinsel. *Tag:* silver tinsel. *Hackle:* yellow and red mixed. *Wing:* yellow feathers inside orange, jungle cock.

Trinity: *Body:* red wool. *Tail:* teal flank. *Ribbing:* silver tinsel. *Tag:* silver tinsel. *Hackle:* red. *Wing:* gray hackle feathers, jungle cock.

Wesley: *Body:* silver tinsel flat. *Tail:* golden pheasant. *Ribbing:* silver tinsel, oval. *Hackle:* black. *Wing:* white bucktail under gray, jungle cock.

White Marabou: *Body:* silver tinsel. *Hackle:* red, under only. *Wing:* white marabou, peacock overlay.

Yellow Marabou: *Body:* silver tinsel. *Hackle:* red outside of wing. *Wing:* yellow marabou, peacock overlay.

How Many Flies?

There is no limit to the number of flies that will be useful in California trout waters. An angler who ties his own flies can merely capture a few insects when he is on the stream and tie reasonable imitations on the spot. The choice is more difficult and much more expensive for anglers who do not tie their own flies. If an angler chooses about a dozen patterns that are standard to fly fishing across the country, he will have imitations of California insects in the vast majority of cases. Again, the size is more important than any other element in fly selection.

Dry Flies

Here are a dozen standard dry and wet flies that will suit most situations.

Dry Flies	Hook Sizes
Adams	10 to 22
Cahill	10 to 18
Royal Coachman	10 to 16
Bivisible	10 to 16
Muddler	6 to 12
Wulff	8 to 12
Dun	10 to 16
Variant	12 to 18
Spider	12 to 20
Deer Hair	10 to 18
Quill	10 to 20
Black Gnat	8 to 22

Wet Flies	Hook Sizes
Leadwing	10 to 16
Black Gnat	8 to 20
Wooly Worm	8 to 16
Dun	10 to 16
McGinty	10 to 14
Royal Coachman	10 to 14
Gray Hackle	10 to 20
Stonefly	10 to 20
Gordon	10 to 16
March Brown	10 to 18
Hendrickson	10 to 18
Inch Worm	10 to 14

Buying Flies

When buying flies from this selection of standard patterns it is better to choose a single dark pattern and a single bright pattern and buy flies in all sizes, rather than to buy one of each different pattern. A Black Gnat or Wooly Worm would be a good choice for the dark pattern and the Hendrickson would be a good choice in the wet fly series. In the dry fly series an Adams and a Black Gnat would be good choices. If money is a real item of importance choose Bivisible in bright and dull colors.

Floating Flies

There are times when floating flies are the only thing trout will accept. The general idea of having flies of many different types and sizes has been discussed. At best the dry fly fisherman should always try to determine what the trout are feeding on, then try to match this food with a fly of the same size and color. This is particularly important during the summer months when the water is clear and trout can inspect a fly closely. In dry fly fishing on rough-water sections of streams size and floatability are more important than any other element.

Flying Ant: *Body:* peacock hurl rear half, tying thread front half. *Hackle:* black. *Wing:* white duck sections.

This is an example of a fly used to imitate a specific terrestrial insect. When ants or termites are swarming, trout often gorge on them and will feed on nothing else. Peacock hurl makes excellent, realistic body material.

Black Gnat: *Body:* black tying thread, shaped. *Tail:* black hackle fibres. *Hackle:* black. *Wing:* black hackle tips.

This is a key pattern and is included here to show about the right amount of hackle. Most commercial flies are tied with far too much hackle.

Fore and Aft: *Body:* peacock hurl. *Hackle:* white front, brown rear. *Tag:* gold tinsel, flat.

This is a basic pattern that is very effective on nearly all streams and particularly on lakes where a Bivisible appears too bulky. Like a Bivisible it is a very floatable pattern and the placement of the hackle allows this fly to stand up on any surface.

Hendrickson: *Body:* animal fur. *Tail:* brown hackle. *Hackle:* cream. *Wings:* hair fibres, divided.

A good all-around fly for small-

er sizes. This fly is a high floater and is very effective for stream fishing where currents are moderate to rough.

Quill: *Body:* quill, dark. *Tail:* white hackle. *Hackle:* white. *Wings:* mallard flank, divided.

A good all-around pattern.

Fox: *Body:* gray animal fur. *Tail:* gray hackle. *Hackle:* gray. *Wings:* brown fox.

This illustrates a western tie for rough-water fishing. Fur body material is very floatable. When properly treated with floatant it will actually bob back to the surface after being drowned in rough currents.

Deer Hair: *Body:* hollow animal hair. *Tail:* bunched animal hair. *Hackle:* brown. *Wing:* animal hair, divided.

This illustrates an excellent type of fly tied with floatability in mind for western streams. All components of the fly are floatable. The body is formed by tying the hair on at the rear end then pulling it forward and tying off at the front.

Pink Bivisible: *Body:* alternate hurl and pink chenille. *Hackle:* gray rear, brown front. *Tail:* gray.

This is a simple pattern that doesn't represent any particular insect but is effective in a specific area. The north fork of the Feather River is where this fly originated.

Spent: *Body:* peacock hurl. *Tail:* few hollow hair spires. *Wing:* hollow hair. *Head:* red.

This fly is included merely to show what can be done with spent fly patterns. The idea is to have plenty of different flies to offer trout during all of the insect life stages, so there are endless variations on this single theme.

Where to Catch Trout

There is no lack of places where you can catch trout in California. For those new to trout fishing or those new to the state a brief outline of trout opportunities is in order. Look over the maps included in this section. They show the major fishing waters in trout country. I've also included a map showing the vast tracts of land in California that are public property.

The land shown in tone is owned by agencies of the Federal government. Most is either Bureau of Land Management or Forest Service land; the rest National Parks, monuments and military reservations. What this points up, I think, is that the same areas that offer our best trout fishing are also the lands open to the public.

Private Lands

There are also areas of private ownership within the public holdings. In California, however, there has been a tradition of allowing public access to huge and important areas. These vast tracts of land are owned by public utilities, railroads and many lumber companies.

Not every company goes along with this tradition, but enough of them do to state that for all practical purposes the public has access to a great deal more than publicly-owned lands. This is an important "plus" for the trout fisherman.

Far North Waters

In the far north state, north of a line from east to west approximately at Red Bluff, there are several important lakes and streams. The main drainages in this area include the Sacramento, Pit and Klamath rivers. The Klamath can be excluded from this trout guide. It is primarily a steelhead and salmon fishery below Iron Gate Dam. Copco Lake is

open to the public and is a very good trout fishery but the premium area above the lake is not open to the public.

Sacramento and Pit Rivers

The Sacramento and Pit rivers form a blue ribbon trout fishery. Trout fishing in huge Shasta Lake is very high quality. At Shasta you can take many fine strings of kamloops rainbow and brown trout by trolling, casting or bait fishing.

In the same drainage are the upper Sacramento River and the McCloud River. Both of these elegant mountain streams are among the finest trout waters in the West. Each also has a small reservoir with a good trout population: McCloud Reservoir and Siskiyou Reservoir. (These rivers are discussed in detail further on in this book.) There are many reservoirs in the high plateau

In a good morning of fishing the lakes and streams in this guide, the angler can expect to take plenty of good trout. By keeping the larger trout and releasing the smaller the angler can end up with some fine strings of fish.

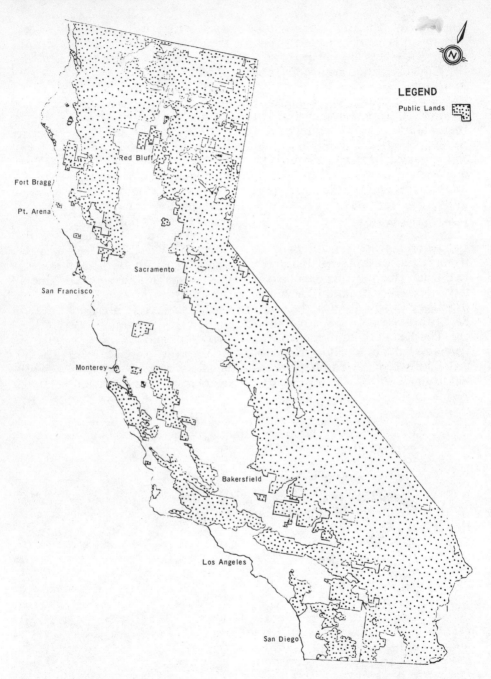

LEGEND

Public Lands

Red Bluff

Fort Bragg

Pt. Arena

Sacramento

San Francisco

Monterey

Bakersfield

Los Angeles

San Diego

Federal Public Lands
of California

country of Modoc and Lassen counties that have trout in them in the Pit River drainage.

Eagle Lake is a special fishery. At this lake only the Eagle Lake Rainbow can survive in the highly alkaline water. The lake is famous for these large trout. The limit is three at Eagle Lake, which upsets some fishermen. It shouldn't. Very few Eagle Lake trout are under two pounds. (This lake is also discussed in detail in this book.)

Lake Almanor

Lake Almanor and the north fork of the Feather River form an extensive fishery in Plumas County. The north fork of the Feather River is one of the finest fisheries in the country. It features fishing in tiny spring-fed creeks that provide ideal brook fishing year around, even in summer. Warm weather doesn't affect them very much. (These streams are covered in detail in this book.)

North Sierra

It would be impossible to mention all the trout fishing water in the High Sierra north of Lake Tahoe. There are hundreds, if not thousands, of lakes in this area. The drainages of several major streams like the Feather, Yuba, Bear, American and Rubicon rivers all have their headwaters in the High Sierra. I included just a few of these lakes in the section on the North Sierra, those in the area of the forest land just north of Interstate 80. All the streams and lakes at these high altitudes—along with their feeder streams—are trout fisheries.

Lake Oroville

Lake Oroville, like Lake Shasta, is a huge and unique lake. In the fall and winter thousands of trout are taken from Oroville. At present kamloops rainbows and browns are the major fish taken at this low elevation lake. Each of the forks of the Feather River above the lake is noted for high-quality trout fishing.

Yuba River

The Yuba River drains an extensive high mountain area. Virtually all the flow in this mighty river system has been altered and dammed. Only a few of the many reservoirs are shown on the map. In the very high mountains are fine Alpine lakes. In fact, the high country is virtually laced with scenic little lakes that have outstanding trout fishing. Most of the high lakes are located over 5000 feet. This makes them ideal for summer fishing.

American River

The American River is another river that drains a lot of country. Like the other streams it is dotted with power-making and irrigation reservoirs. Each of these have trout. Folsom Lake, almost in the state capital, has excellent trout fishing. The lakes and sections of stream in the upper American and Rubicon basin are among the most productive and scenic areas in the world. At the headwaters, in the remote Desolation Wilderness Area, trout fishing almost takes a back seat to the majestic rise of granite mountains towering thousands of feet in the air. Taking handsome native trout in such a setting can have no price tag.

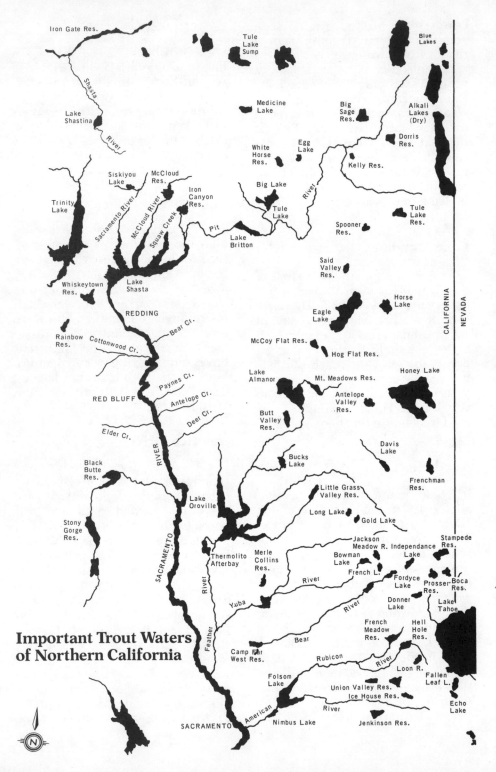

Important Trout Waters of Northern California

Lake Tahoe

Lake Tahoe is special. It is one of the two California lakes that have lake trout. Although thousands of people visit Tahoe each week throughout the year only a few stop off to sample the excellent fishing to be found in the lake. The feeder streams to the lake, and from it, make up some of the best trout water in this part of the state. There are some excellent trout fishing opportunities in this basin.

Mother Lode Trout

South of Lake Tahoe are the many Mother Lode lakes of river systems of the Mokelumne, Calavaras, Stanislaus, Tuolumne, and Merced rivers which all head up in high country. These rivers are long and drain a massive area of high country. Each has been manipulated by power and irrigation interests. Each has excellent trout opportunities relatively close to population centers in the Bay Area. These rivers drain a very high mountain range. Trout fishing is not only good in this area but the grandeur of the country is as fine as any in the world.

San Joaquin River

All of the rivers in the Mother Lode country were originally a part of the extensive San Joaquin River drainage. The headwaters of this completely dammed river system, once the equal of the Sacramento River, have ideal mountain lakes. The country at higher altitudes is breathtaking.

Eastern Sierra

The rivers of the eastern Sierra are the only ones in California that drain east into Nevada. The Carson and Walker rivers are ideal roadside trout waters. They are both picture book streams. This was originally the country of the cutthroat trout. Now the species is limited to a few sections. The rainbow has now replaced the cut as the region's fish.

Crowley Lake is the trout hole most famous in the Owens River basin. Although the Owens is a great trout stream in its own right, Crowley Lake gets most of the publicity from this basin. The reason Crowley is world-famous is because each year it is the scene of a mass invasion of anglers, mostly from southern California. You can nearly walk across the lake on boats on opening weekend. Does this make for poor fishing? No. Each year Crowley delivers tons on tons of trout to avid anglers.

Colorado River

Although it's not shown on the maps, the Colorado River is such a unique river it should be mentioned. The Colorado forms the southeastern state line of California and it offers trout fishing of high quality in a desert setting. The many miles of reservoirs have brought year-around trout fishing to an area that had no good trout fishing in the past. It is a unique thing to be able to take good trout in 100 degree weather.

3500 Trout Lakes!

Even from this sketchy outline of

Important Trout Waters of Central California

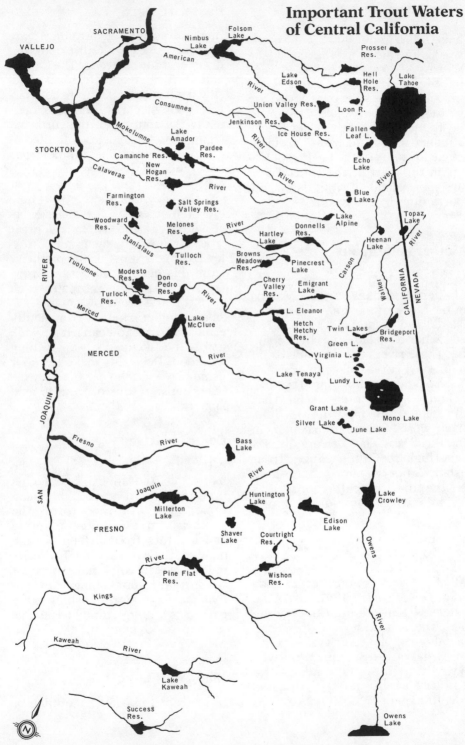

trout possibilities, a reader can see there is no shortage of places to catch trout. The variety of experiences the California trout fisherman can explore is far greater than those found in any other state. There are about 4000 lakes in California. The vast majority, about 3500, have trout.

Stream Trout Fishing

More than anything else, California has lost from its extensive and continuing damming program miles of good fishable trout streams. Nearly all our remaining streams have ready access, usually from roads that run along their banks. Where once your main problem was getting to the streams, now your problem is finding sections of the stream where the quality of fishing hasn't been diminished by other fishermen. Are these areas available? I think so. But a modern angler has to learn some new skills in order to be consistently successful with the conditions we find on California streams today.

California Is Different

When fishing our streams in California it is necessary to change some of the rules we've all learned in the past. The vast majority of our angling literature in the United States has come from the pens of writers on the East Coast. I've read a great deal of it and found it simply does not relate to conditions existing in California. No place on the East Coast (or in most of the West and Midwest) do you have a situation where virtually all streams have their headwaters at an altitude close to 10,000 feet and the lower ranges at sea level.

Underwater Feed

In California waters the type of feed most important to trout is vastly different from that found in other parts of the country. In most drain-ages the stonefly is one of the most important types of underwater feed. It is closely followed by the the caddis fly. There has been a great deal written about the fabulous fly hatches like the so-called "salmon fly" hatches. It's easy to grow lyrical about these massive hatches of spectacular insects. But the hatches of lesser stoneflies and big caddis hatches go nearly unreported.

There are very few flies, for instance, in the average book on flies and fly tying that relate to the California situation. You can certainly take trout in California on flies like the Leadwing Coachman, Iron Blue Dun and McGinty but you are really asking the trout to eat something

In larger streams trout can be found in side currents. Many tributary streams to large lakes have good trout.

that must seem weird to them. In the case of lure fishing in streams, I am relatively certain that about the only things we offer our trout are imitations of baitfish and perhaps frogs or tadpoles. The vast insect world underwater is completely ignored, probably because it would be so difficult to design a lure that looks like most of what is actually there for the trout to eat.

Bait Fishing

I've often wondered about bait fishing. The vast majority of all California trout taken from streams are taken on either salmon eggs or worms. I've cut open and examined thousands of trout and I've never found anything that resembled either of these baits. I've experimented with bait and compared fishing results in the same streams using natural baits found in the stream. The number of trout taken in a given length of time on bait natural to the stream was about one and a half times the number taken on baits not native to the stream.

The only reason I can see to use worms and eggs is their convenience. It does take a bit of extra work to collect stream baits. But I think when you have a stream that has caddis worms on most of the rocks it certainly would seem to make sense to use them. They are much more effective than prepared or unnatural baits.

Caddis fly baits are easy to get. You will see the case worms on the rocks in nearly any riffle and you can merely reach down and pluck them off. You can use the worm's case and all or break the case and rig the worm or several worms on a light wire hook of about No. 12 in size. If you use light line only a few split shot need be added for additional casting weight.

I have nothing at all against bait fishing other than the time it consumes. Every time you stop to put on another bait you are losing all too short fishing hours. Also, it is difficult to cover a lot of water effectively with baits. Probably the top angler in nearly every area is a true bait fisherman. Usually he's also a local angler who is intimately familiar with that particular stream. I don't believe visiting anglers ever stand much chance of being really effective with baits, simply because they can't spend enough hours on a given stream to get to know it really well.

The majority of all anglers are handicapped in stream fishing because they don't have the time to get to know the stream well. To a great extent the visiting angler can change this situation.

Rocky Sections

There are extensive sections of nearly all California streams that rarely, if ever, get fished. These are the sections of rivers and creeks with the white pocket water of riffles and small pools. Typical of all our streams that flow west from the Sierra, and most of the ranges of the far north, is a streambed made up primarily of rocks. Lava rock is a feature of so many streams in California's north state that it can be said to be the rule rather than the exception to find rivers with these features. Visiting anglers can put this factor to work.

Check the stomach contents of all the trout you take, even the little ones like these. This is the key to consistent trout fishing.

Aggressive Wading

The key to successful stream fishing in hard-fished waters like those in California is aggressive wading. It is really amazing how an angler properly fitted with chest high waders with carpet soles and a good wading staff can breast heavy currents. (See "Equipment for Trout Fishing.") In my own fishing I've found I am able to push through fast moving water where it pinches between big midstream rocks. Often these violent currents will be higher than hip deep. With the staff for support you can carefully handle water this deep and fast flowing.

Is Wading Worth It?

Is it worth it? I think so. I've lost count of the number of times I've fished roadside waters this way and have taken good numbers of trout. The importance of aggressive wading cannot be overstressed. If an angler merely wades along the edges of the stream, even with a staff and altered waders, he will do little better than an angler who merely fishes from the bank.

The objective of aggressive wading is to put the angler in exactly the right place in the stream to make short accurate casts to trout holding in the pockets of water be-

Wading up the middle of a river like this is the best way to take a good limit of trout. This is aggressive wading.

hind sunken or partially sunken boulders. There is a pocket of almost dead water directly behind rocks or other obstructions where trout hold. The only way these areas can be fished is to get into perfect position before even making a cast. This applies to using baits or flies. Lures cannot be fished effectively at all in these sections of streams.

In effect, what aggressive wading does for the angler is open up entire sections of streams to careful fishing that can be reached in no other way. The reason shore anglers or timid waders cannot fish these pockets of dead water is that when they make a cast, even one accurate enough to cover the pocket water, the line falls on intervening cur-

rents. The drag against the line whips a fly or bait out of the hole before it ever gets a chance to sink deep enough to tempt a trout. If a fisherman wades until he is directly, or nearly directly, downstream from the hold behind a midstream obstruction, he can lift the tip of his rod enough to keep the last few yards of line off the water. This allows a fly or bait to sink deep with a natural drift. It is a deadly way to hook trout and it will work on the most sophisticiated trout.

A Wading Tip

Even with proper wading gear and staff it is still possible, even probable, that you will get dunked a few times on each trip to the rugged waters of the McCloud and Sacramento, so I advise you to be ready for this. I always take a plastic sandwich bag and put my wallet in it.

Survey a Stream

An important part of stream fishing, or any fishing, is what I call a pre-fishing survey. This is especially true of streams new to an angler, but it is also true for many fishermen who have been fishing a given stream for years. Each stream is made up of a system of feeder streams, even feeder springs in many cases with tiny waters. It makes sense to move around in these drainages to find the best spots to fish. The pre-fishing survey can be as simple as merely driving around in the area of a stream and looking over the types of water available. Binoculars often come in handy, too, when you are scouting for unfrequented water (see "Equipment for Trout Fishing").

Ignore the Easy Spots

As a general rule if a section of stream is very easy to get to, it probably has been fished a great deal, except if it has a lot of wild pocket water. If you find a section of stream where the road runs right to the stream edge you will probably also find a well-worn path along the bank. You might get some effective

The only way you can reach the pockets in a situation like this is with aggressive wading.

Deep wading and long casts are often the only way you can cover the water on larger streams.

fishing if you merely wade the stream and fish from the opposite bank. I would suggest this only if there is no other alternative. A better bet would be to find a section not heavily fished or easy to get to.

In fishing mountain waters I have often found it advisable to find a single spot where access is reasonable and use this spot to penetrate deeper into areas not as easily reached. If an angler never travels around the area drained by a given stream, it is very likely he will miss some of the best fishing potential in that stream system. Some fishermen will fish a stream for years but never stray from the same section. A few miles away there may be a much better stretch of water.

Fly Fishing Gear

I use two fly fishing rigs in my own trout fishing in California. One is built around a 7½ ft. Fenwick rod and the other around an 8½ ft. Fenwick. For fishing small streams like the McCloud or upper Sacramento Rivers the 7½ ft. rod has proved adequate. Fitted with a double taper No. 5 or No. 6 line and a very light Hardy reel this outfit is extremely light and almost casts itself.

I use the larger rig for casting in lakes because it has the backbone to deliver longer casts. In many cases I even change over to Shooting Tapers to get additional distance. These shooting heads are merely the first 30 ft. of a double taper line cut off and tied to monofilament running line of about 20 lb. test. When I am fishing deep I also use fast sinking lines in order to get down to fishing depths as quickly as possible.

The Sacramento and McCloud Rivers

When it comes to fishing with flies in the Sacramento or McCloud rivers I consider the type of wading gear that you use to be as important, or more important, than the flies or the fly fishing equipment that you use. Both of these streams are fished by a large number of people each year. This means that the rivers are both fished to the point that any area that is both easy to get to and easy to fish has been pretty well worked over by most methods of fishing. This does not mean, however, that the streams still do not have plenty of fish. Actually, there are more fish per mile in these two rivers than in almost any other stream that I can name. The trick here is to fish them correctly.

The wading equipment that I use consists of chest high waders that come up under my armpit and carpet-soled wading shoes. I also insist on using a wading staff because with a wading staff you can nearly wade up the middle of the riffle and pocket water sections of the stream, where, if you do not use a staff, you could not get at the bet-

Often, large, deep rivers can be fished only from shore. In this situation spinning gear may be the best choice.

ter pockets of water behind the boulders. Even if you can't wade the stream at all spots you can utilize the wading staff to work your way into the proper spot to make a cast to the holding water behind boulders.

Two Fly Casts

When fishing these two rivers I use a two fly cast on my own terminal rig and I use a 9 ft. leader. The tippets are tapered to 4 lb. test for most of my own fishing, except when I have to go to very small flies like No. 16 to No. 20 sizes, then I change to 2 lb. test tippets. A 2 lb. tippet is tender gear for rough streams like these, however. With a two fly cast you have twice as much going for you as with a single fly on the end of the line. I have even noticed that the trout will change their preference in both of these streams from one time of the day to another, so I usually leave the second and different fly on the other tippet even though I am taking nearly all of the fish on a single fly.

With fly fishing gear I normally only fish the white water riffles that have a lot of boulders and pocket water. As I move down the stream I will make a few casts into the deeper pools and slow moving runs of water, but I feel this kind of water is better fished with light spinning gear rather than with flies. And, very probably, as the season wears on, many other anglers have already fished these easy spots.

The main reason for going through the trouble of wading these deep pocket sections of the stream is that there is no other way to fish them correctly. If an angler tried to fish these sections from shore the currents between the shore and the pocket of water will whip a fly, lure or bait out of the pocket before it ever gets a chance to sink down to the level of the fish. But with proper wading techniques you can put a short cast fly into this water and let it swirl around and sink deep. I hold most of the leader and all of the line out of the water whenever I can in this kind of fishing. I see few other anglers fishing these streams in this way, so if you try this method you'll actually be fishing what amounts to virgin water in the vast majority of cases.

Keep Moving

I have watched literally thousands of anglers fishing both of these rivers with bait of various kinds and few of them do a talented job of it. In most cases these bait fishermen will find a big, deep hole and then merely fish there for hours on end. Both of these rivers are so small that this cannot possibly be the right way to go about bait fishing. After fishing a single hole for no more than 15 minutes with a specific method or type of bait, the angler has either caught the trout that were willing to take that method or bait or the trout in that spot will not yield to this particular method or bait.

The type of bait an angler chooses doesn't make nearly as much difference to success for a day of fishing as what he does with the bait. And if an angler will merely keep on the move and fish many different sections of the stream he has automatically upped the odds on offering the bait to more willing fish than the angler who only fishes a single hole or the holes and riffles in a small part of the stream.

The McCloud River

The McCloud River, located along Highway 89 near the town of McCloud, is included in this trout fishing guide because it is such a classic and prolific stream. In the short stretches of the McCloud River open to the general fishing public the serious trout fisherman will find virtually every type of water that holds trout.

In the headwaters where it is formed by the confluence of several small creeks near Colby Meadows, the McCloud is virtually a creek instead of a river. Here, in a large meadow the angler will find that many areas of the stream are almost standing bodies of still water. In between these big, still pools the river alternates as a brushy pasture stream and then runs over short sections of gravel, sand and lava rock.

McCloud River Access

The McCloud River road and access is the most difficult of any presented in this fishing guide. The bulk of the upper river where the angler will be fishing is owned by private industry which is actively lumbering the

Lower Falls on the McCloud River carries a lot of water from the upper river during spring runoff. Most of the flow of water in the McCloud River comes from spring-fed creeks. Just below Lower Falls is Big Springs, where the size of the river nearly doubles.

land. In each area the fisherman will be forced to double check the roads indicated on the McCloud River map at the time he is on the stream. In general, only roads that have been in passable condition for several years are indicated. Specifically, each road for fishing access has been driven in order to determine if it is passable for the average vehicle. Roads or access points that can only be reached by four wheel drive vehicles or with trail bikes are not included because the majority of anglers do not own these types of vehicles.

Many of the roads are relatively rough for the average automobile or pickup camper because they were made by fishermen just working their way down to the river. But all of these roads are in active use. A typical situation is found in the road system between Fowler Campground and Cattle Camp. Here the main travel road is a heavy duty lumber road that runs east and west and roughly parallel to the main Highway 89. The access roads that lead down to the river are mostly just rough roads that were once used for lumbering operations and are kept passable only because fishermen continue to use them.

In this area, between Fowler Camp and Cattle Camp there is an access road at about a one half to one mile interval. This is typical of the upper river in general, as the reader can tell from the map. But few of these roads are maintained by the Forest Service or the owners of the property.

The best bet for the angler wanting to work these areas is to spend the first day or so of his fishing trip driving down these short roads. In my own case I even take the time to mark the roads that lead to the type of water that I want to fish. I usually mark the good roads for my type of fishing with a pile of stones. However, recently I have found that other anglers will come along and kick these piles over and I changed to marking the roads with a strip of colored plastic ribbon. You may even be able to see some of these rock piles and ribbons still marking the better areas and access roads of the river when you make your own trip to the McCloud River, providing that other anglers have not removed these marking devices.

In most cases the Forest Service has been diligent in putting up signs in most areas to aid the angler in gaining access, but when they are on private land, such as is found at the McCloud River, the signs are relatively scarce and many of them are located out on the highway rather than on the secondary roads. So they are of little use to the angler gaining access from the secondary roads.

Algoma Camp

Near the small campground at Algoma the McCloud begins to gather muscle as more creeks, tiny springs and seeps join the flow of the river. The river runs through a small canyon here and this section is noted for the fact that it has gouged holding pools from the rocks and that just below Algoma the stream enters another flat valley or meadow. The main features of the stream are all but hidden because heavy brush comes right down to the water's edge.

Upper Falls

A short distance below Lakin Dam

the McCloud dives into a relatively deep lava rock canyon to take on the form that most anglers know on the McCloud. Between Lakin and the first falls there is a short stretch of beautiful water that can be quartered by even a modest caster and this area features deep riffles and many long, swift pools that are excellent holding water for larger trout.

Below Upper and Middle Falls there are huge, deep holes that can be worked with any type of equipment. Lures are effective in these deep holes, but probably most of the trout taken from these pools are taken from baits of one kind or another. At Upper Falls the entire flow of the river is pinched into a narrow crevice only a few feet wide. The river falls perhaps 30 feet here and provides some spectacular sights as well as some excellent fishing.

Fowler Camp

Fowler Camp is the only really organized campground provided by the Forest Service in the entire upper river. The river between Middle Falls and Lower Falls, just below Fowler Camp, is classic fly and bait water. The river rushes against huge lava rocks that form the bottom here and the cutting action of the water has gouged out deep holding pockets behind the larger rocks. There is plenty of holding water for the fisherman to work because the river has grown in size enough by this time to provide a very substantial flow of water. You can consistently show here with limits of 12 inch trout if you work the water behind these larger rocks. In the more open flows and smaller pockets there are endless numbers of smaller trout to be taken with flies or baits. In some areas where larger pools have formed, it even makes sense to fish with lures in this section of stream. Until the river reaches Middle Falls, there is hardly enough flow and deep enough water for effective lure fishing, except in the short section from Upper to Middle Falls.

Bigelow Meadow

In the area near Bigelow Meadow the stream has gathered considerable size. In most areas in this section it is difficult to get to the water's edge because the stream is split into many channels and it is beginning to get much deeper. In the area just above Bigelow Meadow beaver dams hold some of the best brown trout in the entire river. However, trying to take these big browns and the big rainbows that also lurk here is a very definite test of an angler's skill. The water of the ponds is still, deep and extremely clear throughout the entire season and to approach a trout in this kind of water is very difficult.

Lakin Lake

Lakin Lake is a small, marshy body of water formed behind Lakin Dam, a standby water supply for the town of McCloud. No boats are allowed on the lake and very little of the shoreline is accessible to the fisherman. However, Lakin does provide deep, cool water needed by larger trout. Fishing just above the flooded area along the big bend that the river makes just before entering Lakin Lake will produce some of the largest fish in the upper river. These larger fish hold in Lakin and often

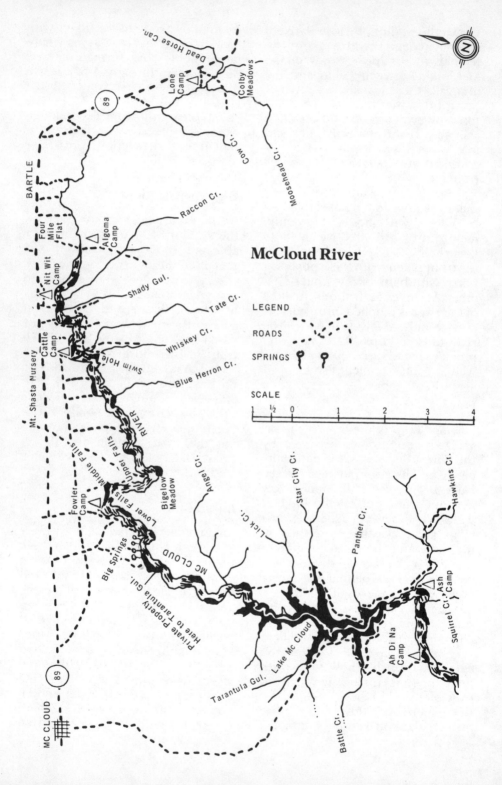

McCloud River

LEGEND

ROADS

SPRINGS

move into this big bend area when they want to feed. Both browns and rainbows can be taken here.

Cattle Camp

Near Cattle Camp the river begins to come into its own because several sizable tributaries enter it from the south, where a long, rolling valley of heavy soil provides a streambed for these little creeks. Even here the McCloud is still a small river that features long, gliding pools and short riffles that connect the pools or that split up to work among the standing brush of the streamside and streambed. Some interesting fishing can be done in these smaller channels where it is necessary to make a careful approach to this area of extremely clear and quiet water.

Big Springs

There is some ideal water between Fowler Camp and Big Springs that can be fished with any method and with any baits, lures or flies. At Big Springs an entire river literally gushes from the lava-rock sides of the McCloud River canyon wall. The McCloud River actually more than doubles in size at Big Springs and you can see the masses of water gushing out of the lava rocks in several different places. There is an old abandoned pumphouse located over the largest of the springs. When you spot this small shack you know you've located Big Springs.

Some of the largest trout in the McCloud River hold in the area for the next mile or so below Big Springs. The springs provide a year around flow of icy cold water that is absolutely perfect for trout. The main river provides an endless flow of food and plant material from where it has run through the fertile valley and meadow areas upstream. The combination of perfect water temperature and food filled water is what causes the trout to hold in this area.

Private Property

A short distance below Big Springs the river banks are posted and anglers cannot gain access except through permission from the landowners.

McCloud Reservoir

McCloud Reservoir, or Lake McCloud, is located a few miles below Big Springs. Fishing is allowed on this lake even though it is located on private property. Camping is allowed at Star City Creek and launching is from four rough launch sites, located at Tarantula Gulch where the road approaches the lake, at Battle Creek where there are limited parking facilities, near the dam where a very rough launch site is available and where Star City Creek comes into the lake.

In general, fishing is permitted on this lake in the area from Tarantula Gulch to Star City Creek access point for shore fishermen. However, the banks of the lake are very steep in most places and only a few spots allow comfortable bank fishing. I consider this a boat fishing lake. I have had my best luck fishing near the feeder streams, particularly the area where the McCloud River enters the lake. I used quick sinking wobbling spoons to fish but baits of any kind are good in this area. Larger trout of up to 6 pounds are available and taken regularly from this part of the lake.

On the map provided here I have noted the old river channels for the angler who wants to troll McCloud Lake. By trolling these areas the angler is better off than to merely troll at random.

Ash Camp

Signs provided by the Forest Service at Lake McCloud say that the nearest public camp is located at Ah Di Na Meadows, but there are several rough campsites on Forest Service land at Ash Camp, right at the mouth of Hawkins Creek. The road to this camp is passable even with a passenger car and if the angler is equipped to camp without need for running water, he can use this camp instead of having to travel clear to Ah Di Na Meadows Campground every day.

There is some very fine pocket and deep pool water in the area near Ash Camp that holds some large trout. However, when fishing this area the angler should be very careful if he does any wading. The PG&E power operations from McCloud Dam are very erratic and the flow of water can be changed in an instant making wading, particularly deep wading, very dangerous for about three miles below the dam site. Here it is better to use lures or fish baits and flies while not wading.

Ah Di Na Meadows

Some of the biggest trout in the McCloud River can be taken from the deep holes located between Ash Camp and Ah Di Na Meadows Camp. These deeper sections are best fished with either bait or with lures that will run deep.

I like to fish Ah Di Na Meadows in the fall of the year when the flow here is at a minimum. Most of the water coming down the river goes into a diversion tunnel three miles below the dam and the flow at the meadows is relatively consistent year around. You can fish for approximately a mile upstream and half a mile downstream in this area. Below this point the river is privately owned to its confluence with Shasta Lake and this entire area is posted.

A perfect day-long trip can be made fishing from Ah Di Na to Ash Camp. It takes this amount of time to fish the river in this area properly. I generally fish upstream, starting at Ah Di Na and fish toward Ash Camp where I have my wife pick me up in the evening. An even better trip is to work this area using a light sleeping bag and staying overnight about half way up the stream. For this fishing I use a combination rod that can be used for both fly and lure fishing. The best results here are found in the early morning and late evening hours with the possible exception of the month of October when the fish will hit virtually all day long or on any day that has heavy overcast skies.

Private Property

Much of the finest water on the McCloud River is heavily posted, and in most cases the landowners who have this land posted are very serious about the subject and will prosecute violators. There is one large benefit to having large areas where virtually none of the fish are harvested such as we find at the McCloud River. The low utilization factor for these long stretches of stream allow many trout to attain larger sizes. These fish then tend to migrate into areas where they find less competition from larger fish, such as they will find in areas where the general public harvest a larger percentage of the fish that are in the river. This is one of the factors that contributes, I feel, to the very high quality of the trout fishing found through the lower river up as far as Lower Falls, the upstream barrier to trout migrations.

Another thing to remember when fishing the McCloud is that rainbows from this private and posted land and from Shasta Lake migrate into the stream in the spring in order to spawn. It's a good idea to fish this stream in the lower stretches during the spring and early season months when the number of rainbows has increased to the maximum carrying capacity of the water. In the fall brown trout migrate into this section of the stream to spawn and this population is as high as it is going to get during the month of October.

Checking the Water

I have skin dived with mask and snorkel in many areas of the McCloud River and have found that the fish are more numerous than you would think for a relatively small stream such as this. In probing the deeper holes I have found

that the larger brown trout are generally out of the current and hold in the waters that are well protected from the current. They have a penchant for holding under the cover of the large grass tufts that you will see on the sides of the stream and even in the middle of the stream where it is possible for them to gain a foothold. I have found that casting a fly to these grass clumps and allowing it to sink down in the dead pockets of water right next to where the grass sweeps the current is a very effective way to take brown trout.

The basic items of food for trout of all kinds in the McCloud River are the stoneflies and caddis flies that are very abundant in the stream, and in the many creeks that feed into the river. It is a simple matter to gather a supply of these to use for baits and the caddis worms can merely be plucked from the stones of nearly any riffle. To get the stoneflies just pick up stones and take them off the bottom. Generally the stones in riffles and swiftly moving water are the best spots. In the still waters of a pool you will find very few stoneflies or caddis fly larva.

Using flies that imitate the stonefly and caddis fly are the best bet. This holds true when the insects are hatching. A Sack Fly of about No. 8 size on a long shank hook has been the best fly for my own fishing once the insect hatches are on. You can pluck a few of the flies from the streamside bushes and use these for baits or for imitations to be tied with a fly-tying outfit. Both the stonefly and the caddis are readily visible in the streamside brush at this stage of their development.

Fishing the McCloud

I consider the McCloud River almost entirely a fly or bait fishing stream. Trying to work lures effectively in pocket water such as that from the falls to Ah Di Na Meadows can get to be a very expensive business. The lava rock and small holding pockets of water behind the larger stones are simply not suitable for lure fishing, except in the limited number of places that we have noted.

In the case of fly fishing virtually the entire river can be reached by a competent fly fisherman, providing he is willing to wade aggressively. In order to wade effectively in heavy water such as is found in most of the stretches of the river below the falls, a wading staff is essential. No matter how brave an angler might be, wading without a staff is foolhardy. This is particularly true in the area below Big Springs where the volume of water is such that it is necessary to depend on a wading staff even if you fish only close to the shoreline and wade only in this section of the stream.

For my own fishing I wade until I am in the protection of one of the stream boulders. There is virtually no current in these holding pockets and it is safe to let the staff hang at your side while standing in this quiet water. I then fish all of the pocket water within easy casting distance of where I am standing. I prefer that no line whatever falls on the water when fishing this way and I generally use a 9 to 12 foot leader so that I can have as much free drift as possible. If you hold the fly line well up and the rod tip as high as possible it is even possible to allow a fly to sink straight down the back side of the boulders and tufts of grass. You need not worry about scaring fish from these short distances. In wild, white water, like that in most of the McCloud, the trout cannot see an angler until he is in the same pocket as the trout. In fact, I've often looked down and seen trout finning in the same pocket of water where I was standing, so close that you could reach down and touch them with your hand.

Bait should be fished exactly the same way as a fly. There will be few if any trout in the fast moving white water of the stream and trying to get a bait down in this water is all but impossible. Instead, the angler should fish the same water as is fished with flies, working the baits down the back side of rocks and grass tufts. The best baits are those found in the stream but baits such as worms, salmon eggs and others should still be fished in these pockets of water instead of out in the fast moving currents. The only exceptions are the relatively few deep pools. Then working along the sides and in the deepest part of the pools is in order. In pools trout generally hold when feeding either near the front or the back end of the pool.

Flies for Trout

Virtually any trout fly will work at one time or another in the rivers and lakes in this guide, but in my own experience I have found that using certain patterns is important to success in many cases.

By turning over almost any rock in the stream, the angler can determine just what kind of food is available to the trout in that particular stretch of the stream. These rocks, generally taken from the riffles, will be covered with insect life of one kind or another.

McCloud River Flies

The McCloud River is a classic trout stream. If you turn over almost any stone in the stream you will see why it is such a prolific stream. Smaller stoneflies cling to nearly every rock in the stream and caddis flies of two or three types are available. Flies that imitate these important trout food items are very necessary.

I use Wooly Worms and several different nymph patterns in my own fishing on the McCloud and I have found that it is far better when using these flies to have them either weighted with fuse lead wire or tied on heavy wire hooks so that they will sink quickly in the pocket water. The better trout will always be found in the little still spots behind boulders in this boulder-strewn river. Only heavy flies can sink down deep in this type of water.

There are many mayfly hatches in the McCloud throughout the year and the bulk of them are imitated well with a No. 14 to No. 10 pattern. I use a Pale Evening Dun, a Light Cahill, a Horner Deer Hair or a Brown Bivisible for the bulk of my own dry fly fishing. And even though I prefer to fish with a lightly hackled fly, the McCloud River is such a rough flowing stream that the Bivisibles and deer hair flies do a much better job of floating, even if they do not come as close to imitating the emerging insects. The riffle water is the place to present these flies because the water is so clear during the summer and fall that trout are tough to take in the pools.

Upper Sacramento River

The upper Sacramento River, from where it flows into Shasta Lake to the new Box Canyon Dam and Lake Siskiyou, is a really remarkable trout stream. Even though it flows south right along a steaming freeway, Interstate 5, it provides some of the finest stream fishing for rainbows and occasional brown trout that can be found in California.

This section of the Sacramento River has a particularly steep gradient that causes the stream to have a great number of riffles and fast flowing sections. This means that the fly fisherman who works the river correctly can find plenty of pocket water in the white water sections of the stream.

The country through which the stream flows is basically rocky and through the years the stream has gouged out many deep pools where the larger trout can be taken by either fly or lure fishermen. Some of the deeper pools go from 20 to 40 feet in depth, although the average pool will be closer to perhaps 15 feet in depth.

Kinds of Fishing

Of course, you can always use just

The Sacramento River starts at high elevation at a series of runoff lakes that are extremely scenic. Here the author is fishing Cedar Lake with the assistance of his Brittany spaniel.

about any type of equipment that is suitably light for trout fishing, but this particular section of the Sacramento River is best suited for either fly fishing or bait fishing. If an angler decides to use lures he will have to stay on his toes in order to avoid losing a lot of gear because the river changes rapidly almost mile by mile —and even within a few hundred yards—from deep holding water to relatively shallow riffles. To work the river properly the lure fisherman should have a good selection of lures that work well in all types of water.

Access

As in fishing any new stream, or any new section of a stream, fishing this section of the Sacramento River between Shasta and Siskiyou lakes presents a problem of access to the river. Even though the river is serviced by a superhighway, which runs along right next to the stream, this does not mean that there is free and open access down the bank to the river. It would certainly be wrong for an angler to merely park his car on the shoulder of the highway and scale down to the water. It would also be illegal. But even if it were legal, the canyon through which the river runs is so steep that you'd virtually need a scaling rope to get to the water.

For the first-time angler on the Sacramento it is of value to use the notes I have compiled on access roads and routes in the following. By using these notes you will be able to do more fishing and less searching for ways of getting down to the water.

Owner Access

A great deal of the access to the river is over Southern Pacific Railroad property, and in some cases through other ownership. In the past, except for a few instances, these streamside land owners have permitted the fishermen to get to the river in the most logical way. So, it behooves all of us to prevent litter and any other unreasonable invasion of these properties. In fact, if I see litter in this area I clean it up myself because I want to continue to fish the area in the future.

Dog Creek Access

The first Interstate 5 interchange above Shasta Lake that is of interest to the trout fisherman is the Dog Creek or Vollmers turnoff. At this freeway turnoff the road to the east leads down to the town of Delta. There are only a few parking spots here and access is through the railroad yard to the river. A better bet is to take the Dog Creek Road over the freeway to the west. Even though it would seem that going west would be wrong, when the river is located to the east, the reason for heading this way is that shortly after the Dog Creek Road heads west of the highway it intersects a Forest Service road that is marked Fender Ferry Road.

The Fender Ferry Road crosses under the new freeway, under the old Highway 99 bridge and across the Sacramento River a short distance from there. There are many parking spaces here.

This section of the river features a good series of holes right at the bridge and also up and downstream from this spot you will find

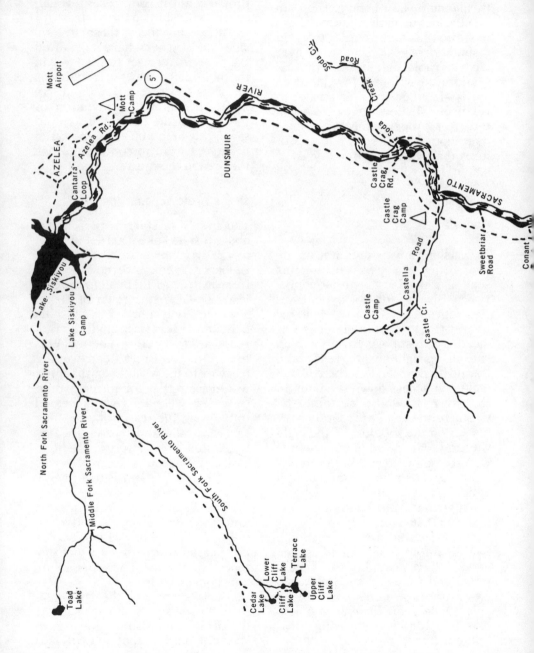

Sacramento River

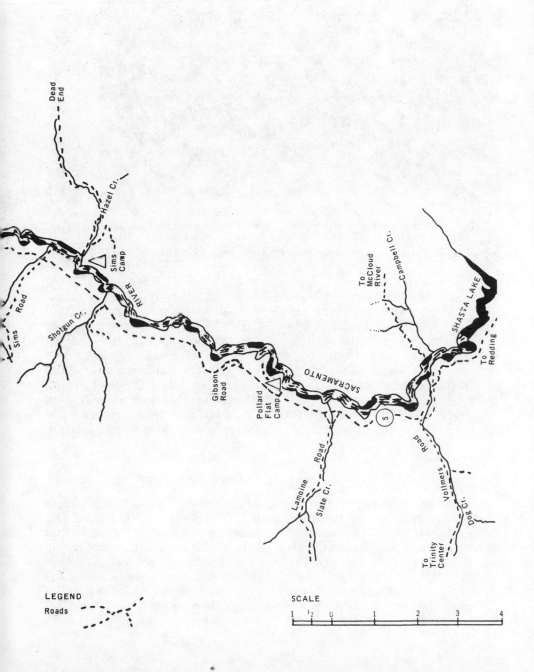

LEGEND

Roads

SCALE

1 1 2 0 1 2 3 4

Dog Creek access road turns back from the east and crosses the Sacramento River after passing under the freeway and under the old highway bridge. There is an excellent selection of deep holes downstream from this spot and good riffle water above.

good pool water interspersed with riffle water, at any stage of the season. This area is particularly good in the spring and again in the fall for spawning trout that have come upstream from Shasta Lake. In the spring the rainbows will be in the river for spawning and in the fall the larger brown trout use this and other sections of the river.

LaMoine Road Access

The next upstream — north — access road for the Sacramento River is the LaMoine Intersection exchange. Access here is west off Interstate 5 and the road crosses under the freeway. Access is across the Southern Pacific tracks.

This area also features a selection of pool water with white water in between. In general, this section will hold larger trout than most sections of the river because the riffle water is normally much deeper than it is in most of the river. Larger trout prefer these deeper runs of water to the shallower riffles that make up most of the Sacramento River. The pools here are very deep and even lure fishermen can fish this area without having to face too many obstacles.

Pollard Flat Camp

At the Pollard Flat exchange there is a Forest Service campground and access is down a very steep trail that is even marked "Use Caution" by the Forest Service. The steep trail here is worth the effort because of the many deep holes with deep riffles here. These pools are formed because a huge, rocky bluff has been cut away by the river over the years. This is a particularly good lure and bait fishing area because larger fish tend to stay in this section during the summer months because the sun remains on the water for only a short time each day.

A mile or so north of Pollard Flat there is a rough access road that leads to a big flat on a bend in the river that is excellent for both lure or fly fishermen. You can take an automobile down this road even though it looks very rough, if you use caution and don't hurry.

The old highway goes down toward the river and there are access roads to the river a few hundred yards from where the old highway is blocked. There is a single turnaround at the bottom of the rough road but normally it is best to park on the old highway and walk down to cross the S.P. tracks to the river. This area is excellent for lures and flies, especially in the fall months when the water is low.

Gibson Road

Gibson Road, located 1.7 miles north of Pollard Flat, is one of the best all around bait, lure and fly areas in this section of the river. Access is to the east; turn west to a section of old Highway 99.

Railroad Bridge

There is an unmarked access road to one of the best overall fly fishing sections in the entire upper river at a spot where you can see a silver railroad bridge crossing the river. In the spring, at high water, this area can be worked with just about

The Sacramento River is not noted for the number of brown trout that it contains, but when you do manage to net a brown it is usually a fairly good-sized fish. This one came from near the mouth of Dog Creek where a large hole is formed, preferred by browns.

any kind of gear, but in the late summer and fall when the water is running low this area is almost strictly a fly fishing stretch.

Sims Road

At Sims Road the river is reached to the east where a bridge services a large, improved Forest Service camp. This is an excellent fly fishing stretch. In spring lures are good in the deeper runs. The best fly fishing areas are those lined with fairly thick stands of brush, so you must be prepared to wade deeply here to reach the pocket water. At low water this is a poor lure or bait section.

Flume Creek Road

Flume Creek Road leads to heavily posted private property.

Conant Road

On the east side of Conant Road there is a large turnaround and parking area and an old, abandoned bridge that can be used to get access to the east side of the river.

At the bridge and for some length upstream and down there is excellent fly water.

On the west side of Conant Road there is another access road that heads back upstream after the intersection. This road crosses the freeway and leads to an excellent bend in the river that has a lot of fly

A typical section of the Sacramento River just above Sims Camp at spring runoff level. Note how much holding water is formed behind the rocks. The trout will be found just out of the white water in the holes behind the rocks.

water upstream as far as the abandoned bridge mentioned earlier and some good lure and bait holes downstream. Access is along S.P. tracks.

Park with extreme care here so your vehicle will not interfere with railroad operations. The area is not posted yet.

Sweetbrier Road

Sweetbrier Road leads to some excellent fly water. You have to pass through the S.P. facility here to reach the water. Park with care.

Castella Road

At Castella Road you can cross the river at either the regular bridge or at the bridge that leads to Cragview Resort and Trailer Park. This resort is located on the east side of the river and is reached by heading upstream. The second bridge heads due east and leads to a state picnic facility.

On the west shore there is a Frontage Road that follows the river all the way to the Soda Creek Road. There is a footbridge owned by the state a short distance north from the Castella Road access. On this road, that fronts the entire section of river, there is a lot of private property almost all the way north to Dunsmuir, so access should be gained only when the route is not posted.

Dunsmuir

Virtually every road in and near Dunsmuir ends at the river and access here is obvious. This area is fished heavily by the local residents and I normally feel that it is best left for the local people. The chance that a visitor can find willing fish that have been overlooked by the people who live here is very remote.

Mott Azalea Road

A few miles north of Dunsmuir is the Mott Azalea Road. After crossing the S.P. tracks the road that heads west leads to several rough campsites on the ridge above the river. A very rough road leads down the ridge to the river to some excellent fly and lure water but it is doubtful if you should take a passenger car down this road.

The road that heads north at the S.P. track crossing leads to an intersection with the Cantarra Road. The one that leads south at the S.P. track crossing merely makes a big loop and returns where it started. There is a camp on the east side of the freeway.

Cantarra Loop

The Cantarra Loop Road leads to one of the top sections of the Sacramento River. This section of stream has every type of water that you could want. In the fall the fly fishing here can be sensational but you must be willing to wade a great deal. But there are many deep holes and runs of water that can be fished with any kind of equipment. There are a lot of pullouts at the end of the Cantarra Road where a car may be parked. This is the last good access road to the river below Box Canyon Dam where you can drive directly to the river.

In the summer months the angler can wade without wading equipment. Taking some time out to find out what kind of feed is available to the trout is a key to taking the trout in these streams and lakes.

Lake Siskiyou

Lake Siskiyou opened to the public at the beginning of the 1970 fishing season. It is well-stocked by the Department of F&G and features "trophy" trout.

The camping facilities are outstanding at this lake, and it would be well worth choosing either the facility at Region 1 (F&G Dept.) or at Sims Camp Flat for headquarters when fishing the upper Sacramento.

Above Siskiyou

The river changes character a great deal above Lake Siskiyou. This is flood and runoff territory and the river has scoured the stream bed to such an extent that there is not much holding water for larger fish. However, the angler who likes to take smaller trout will find that this is good fishing early and late in the day all through the summer months for these smaller fish.

The road is paved to the ridge along the South Fork and it leads to the headwaters of the South Fork at Cedar and Cliff lakes. These are exquisite little lakes and you should make an effort to at least see and fish them. If you have a small cartop boat, by all means take it along. The trout are generally small but the scenery alone is worth the trip.

Sacramento River Flies

The same flies that work well for me

in the McCloud also do a good job in the Sacramento. Before the dam was built at Lake Siskiyou I found you could generally use larger flies than in the McCloud. Now, however, Siskiyou Lake has formed a settling basin for sediment in the river and the water in the Sacramento is very clear.

The Sacramento is famous for its fall (October) caddis fly hatches. This is a hatch of very large caddis flies that you can see whizzing around at this time of year in droves. This large caddis is also large in its nymph form and you can select samples from nearly any riffle in the lower stream. The trout will usually be gorged with these in-sects either in the nymph form or the adults.

The Sacramento is now at least as clear as the McCloud. Before the dam was built I had my best luck with flies ranging between No. 12 and No. 10, and even No. 8 in some cases, during the late fall, when the caddis were nearing maturity. Now I find smaller flies down to No. 14 work best. If you want to buy really good flies for fishing the Sacramento or the McCloud contact Ted Fay at his Lookout Point Motel in Dunsmuir. Ted is not only a top fly fisherman, who fishes these streams almost daily, but his work on fly development for these two rivers is significant.

Tributaries of the Sacramento River

There are several small tributary streams to this section of the Upper Sacramento River that are well worth the angler's time to fish. In general these six streams are best fished during the early season and early summer months when there is a good flow of water in them. But any time of the year these six streams will have beautiful little rainbow trout and usually some fish planted by the Department of F&G, when it is feasible.

I have rarely found another angler fishing in these streams, with the exception of Castle Creek, which runs through the high-use camping area of Castle Crags State Park. Evidently, when visiting anglers get close to the Sacramento River they feel that their time is bet-ter spent fishing the larger waters of the river rather than to expend their fishing effort in these tiny streams. This is true enough if the size of the fish that the angler wants is the only criterion for his fishing effort. But for the fisherman who likes various kinds of streams and likes to fish in varying types of cover and under conditions which force him to use delicate techniques, the six streams that are tributary to the Upper Sacramento are little jewels.

Size of Fish

I have never personally caught any fish in the streams tributary to the Upper Sacramento that went larger than 12 inches. I suppose that in the deeper holes in the more remote

The trout taken from the small tributary streams to the Sacramento River are generally fairly small fish, but they are beautiful little natives in most cases.

sections of these streams larger fish live, but I consider a 12 inch fish taken from these picturesque little waters at least the equal of an 18 to 22 inch fish taken from the main waters of the river itself.

The average rainbow that I take when I fish these little streams will run from 8 to 10 inches. It is possible with determination to limit up on 10 inch fish, especially in streams of larger size, such as Slate Creek, but I specifically do not pay much attention to size when I fish these streams. Here, it is the quality of the sport rather than the size and quantity of the fish that counts to me.

Access Problems

If you utilize the maps presented in this trout guide, or if you use the free maps that can be obtained from any Forest Service station in this forest, you will see that there are good roads that follow, in general, the course of most of the creeks that are named. However, the canyon of the Sacramento River is an extremely steep one and this makes these roads virtually useless as access roads for the fisherman wanting to fish these small tributaries except in certain sections.

These roads are virtually all general service Forest Service roads. This means that they are normally passable for the average family vehicle or pickup camper. But as they scale the steep ridges of the canyon—to provide Forest Service and lumber access—they begin to climb the flanks of the mountains and this usually takes them away from the creeks that we want to fish. Even though the maps show the roads as still following the general course of the streams, the roads are usually from a few hundred feet to a few thousand feet away from the actual stream bed. Also, these mountains are so steep that you generally cannot scale down the mountain from the roads, even if you were willing to try doing so.

Fish Lower Sections

I have found that it is usually best to gain access to these tributaries in the lower few miles of their course. In the cases where there are access crossings shown it is usually not a good idea to drive out several miles of dusty roads in order to sample the upper sections of these relatively short streams. The streams gain force and flow as they move down the length of the slope from numerous springs that join the main creeks. In most cases the upper sections of all of these streams are very tiny any time of the year except during the spring runoff period. Any trout that are in them the rest of the year will usually leave for the larger downstream sections if they are able.

Wading Necessary

I normally wade in almost all of my own stream trout fishing, but I see most other anglers either not wading at all or only wading on the fringes of the stream. In the case of fishing the feeder streams to the Sacramento, I've found that wading is virtually a necessity just in order to move along the length of the stream as you fish. In most cases the stream itself, or portions of each stream, has thick brush that comes right down to the banks. In many cases this brush and cover is so thick that it is all but impossible to penetrate and the only avenue of progress along the stream is to get into the water.

In most of these streams the angler doesn't have to wade very deep, because, except in the pool sections, the water is not really that deep. And even in the sections that have pools it is often possible to move around the area so that deep wading is not needed. In my own case, when I am fishing the main river here I will always use chest or armpit high waders and carpet-soled wading shoes. In the river I find that I am always at least hip deep in the water. But for fishing the smaller tributaries I generally dispense with the waders and merely use the carpet-soled shoes. In a few cases the angler will need to go hip deep in order to move along the stream but in most cases it is only necessary to go knee deep.

Wading these streams and fighting your way along the brushy sections of them can be fairly strenuous in many cases. This is the reason that I dispense with wearing the heavy waders, which would make the effort just too strenuous. I rarely would use hip boots for fishing this type of situation because in almost every case it would be necessary to wade deeper than hip boots will permit.

Flies and Baits

These small tributary streams are not really suitable for lure fishing in the vast majority of cases. The lure fisherman who is determined can find a few sections of each stream that can be worked effectively with lures, but the pocket water that is common to all of these streams is best fished with either baits or flies.

I checked out the insect life of most of these streams using a wire net that is placed downstream from rocks which are lifted so that insects and nymphs that are washed downstream are trapped against the net by the force of the current. About the only natural baits I found that were large enough to provide baits that could be attached to a hook were caddis flies and a few of the larger nymphs or stoneflies. There were many mayfly nymphs evident in the screenings, but these were all generally too small and too delicate for use as baits. An angler who wants to use natural baits can either collect his baits right on the stream with a net or by merely plucking the caddis—case worms—from the rocks of a riffle.

As an experiment I tried using case worms with case and all and I didn't do very well. I did much better when I stripped the worm from the case and used it in a natural drift with very little weight. In this kind of fishing, during the major part of the season, a No. 14 hook

When sampling the waters with a small sifting strainer it is best to use a white pan to determine what samples of underwater insect life may be present. In the white pan the insects are readily visible whenever they begin to move around.

STREAM TROUT FISHING — 93

with light wire proved best. In the fall when the caddis are nearing maturity a slightly larger hook would be more suitable. Worms or salmon eggs will work, too.

Using Flies

I generally fish these streams with flies exclusively. I have found that flies will take about as many fish as will baits and the fact that I do not have to continually keep rebaiting and changing baits allows me much more time with the fly in the water and fishing than would be the case with any kind of bait. For the bulk of the fishing in these smaller streams I have found that virtually any nymph or Wooly Worm fly in sizes from No. 14 to No. 10 will take these trout. The insect life in the streams is generally dull colored and small and this means that the flies used to represent them should be dull and small.

I found no need to use weighted flies, as is often needed in order to get deep enough in the main river. These streams are relatively shallow and the flow in them, even during the spring, is fairly sedate. Very probably a lightly hackled Wooly Worm in various dull colors is all that is needed for wet fly fishing, but I tested a variety of wet patterns and they all took fish.

Dry Flies

There are an uncommon number of all types of terrestrial insects in the streamside brush of this entire drainage, but the vast number of insects to be found in the streamside brush of these tiny tributaries is really outstanding. Any angler who fishes these streams will discover for himself when he brushes against this streamside brush. In almost every case, even if you are merely moving along the streamside through the brush and broad leaf plants, absolute hordes of insects will fly up when you disturb any of this foliage.

In determining what to use for fishing dry flies I normally first use a short-handled, strong beating net in the streamside brush of each stream for a few minutes to determine what kind of flying insects are available. (See "Equipment for Trout Fishing.") I then use insect imitations that roughly, at least, resemble the type of insects on hand. Once I begin to take trout I inspect the stomach contents and determine what they have actually been eating. This way an angler doesn't have to go through a long process of trial and error in order to begin to take trout with flies, especially floating flies.

In the streamside brush of the Sacramento River and especially the tributary streams I found that there were an uncommon number of different species of small beetles. However, they are generally very small beetles during most of their life cycle. Also, when I examined the stomach contents of several trout I found that they had been eating beetles almost exclusively.

When the brush is struck with a beating net literally hundreds and even thousands of these beetles swarm up. They are not strong fliers and many of them evidently fall to the surface of the water. For this reason I use Jassid flies, which are a good imitation of small beetles and insects. They are very effective almost any time of the day in this

A sturdy beating net is used to take samples of insects from the brush along the shoreline of lakes and streams. There are literally hundreds of different kinds of insects that cannot be seen readily in this brush near the water.

drainage and I use these patterns as my basic dry fly offering.

Along with the beetles and other types of insects there are the normal complement of mayflies in this brush. When a mayfly hatch is coming off the water it is relatively simple to determine what size and color the particular hatch is made up of and imitating the current hatch is advisable, as it would be in any stream fishing for trout. But the beetle imitations proved particularly effective in this particular section of the Sacramento River. But once freezing weather hits this drainage, the effectiveness of Jassid, as well as most other dry flies, is seriously in doubt. At this time of year I change over almost exclusively to wet flies, or try to imitate larger flying insects like the large caddis which hatch in the fall months at just about the time that the first freezes occur in this area.

Dog Creek Access

The first of the year-around tributaries worth considering is Dog Creek. Access to Dog Creek is at Vollmers turnoff from Interstate 5. There is fairly good access to the lower stretches of Dog Creek from the bridges to the east of the highway where the road crosses it.

Dog Creek is one of the most overgrown of the tributaries to the Sacramento, but it is definitely fishable for the angler who is willing to wade—a must here. Dog Creek is a particularly scenic stream for the fisherman willing to dope out how to use his tackle in overgrown waters. In most cases the trees and brush actually come together to form a sort of protected tunnel that spans the stream. Only in a few of the wider areas does the full sunlight fall on this creek in the lower few miles.

Access is blocked by private property for nearly the entire reach of Dog Creek and this property is held by small landowners who have posted the waters against trespassing. This stream is posted upstream to such an extent that Department of F&G rarely stocks it anymore.

Fishing Dog Creek

I generally use a very short, light leader for fishing a situation such as is found at Dog Creek. A leader of 5 or 6 feet tapered to about 1 lb. test proves adequate for this kind of fishing because the casts are rarely more than 10 or 15 feet, including the leader, and with this much line

out a short leader is needed in order to turn a fly over.

The pocket and holding water where the fish hold will be obvious to the angler who fishes the creek. I have found that it is best here to fish only the pocket water and the water at the back ends of any riffles and pools. The bulk of the water is too shallow to hold good trout except during spring runoff.

Slate Creek Access

Slate Creek can be reached by taking the LaMoine exit from the freeway and heading east. The road bends back and crosses the creek here and this is the single best access point for the general public.

Fishing Slate Creek

Slate Creek is one of the larger tributaries to the Sacramento River and it

In the gentler parts of streams the angler should be able to make long casts. Trout are much harder to take in this kind of quiet water than in the white-water pockets where only very short casts are necessary. Early and later in the day are best here.

is also an open stream when compared to streams like Dog Creek or Hazel Creek, further upstream. Fly fishing here can be done with longer and finer leaders in most areas because the wading angler can get a good back cast by working straight up or straight downstream. As the angler fishes upstream it becomes a bit more brushy and it is advisable to change to shorter leaders for the best casting.

Slate Creek has more and deeper riffles than most of the other tributaries and these deeper riffles are worth fishing during early morning and late evening hours. However, the larger resident trout will be found in the pocket water during these periods of the day as well as during the warm parts of the day. This stream produces consistently larger trout than the smaller streams, especially in the area right near the Sacramento River confluence. I prefer fishing standard dry fly patterns here because the streamside brush does not crowd the lower sections of this stream and, being open to the sun, mayfly hatches are regular and numerous.

Hazel Creek Access

Hazel Creek flows into the Sacramento just south of Sims Flat Forest Service Campground. It is serviced by a Forest Service road that crosses it a few miles above Sims Camp. There are also access points and roads on private property owned by the Southern Pacific Railroad. This company does not generally exclude the public from its land and if no littering or excessive camping takes place this should remain ready access to the water.

Fishing Hazel Creek

The situation at Hazel Creek is just about the same as that found at Dog Creek. The stream is brushy right down to the banks and the trees often come together over the stream to form a sort of green tunnel. I use the same techniques and flies with success here.

Hazel Creek has more deep water than Dog Creek and the angler who wades, as he must to fish this stream, will find that he often has to push through chest deep pools. Either that, or he will have to fight his way through thick underbrush and plant life. The stream is very scenic and a classical stream for the angler who enjoys doping out the methods of presentation of flies or baits. Lures are virtually excluded for fishing Hazel Creek.

Shotgun Creek Access

Shotgun Creek can be reached by turning off the freeway at Shotgun Creek Lodge. The lower miles of the stream feature deep pocket water in relatively scoured rock slabs. The stream is actually a series of cascades of water that pour from one rocky pocket basin into another.

This stream is relatively sterile in the lower reaches because there isn't much overhanging brush or trees except in a few spots. However the deeper pockets hold some of the largest trout of any found in the streams tributary to the Sacramento precisely because of the deepness of these pockets. I have had my best success here with wet flies and have rarely been on hand when a sizeable mayfly hatch occurred.

Mears Creek Access

Mears Creek is reached from the east of the highway at Sims Road. This road intersects a portion of old Highway 99 that crosses the lower section of the creek. An access road heads upstream for a half mile and access can be gained from parts of this Forest Service road. Portions of this road are privately owned and posted, but most of the road is not posted.

Mears Creek is much like Shotgun Creek in that it consists of a large number of deep pools pouring one into another. It is a slightly smaller stream than Shotgun most years but it has adequate flow to support the trout that hold in the deeper holes. There is virtually no riffle water on this stream but the pockets and pools are numerous and this is where the trout hold. The stream is scoured and most of the fishing should be done with bait or sinking flies. Weighted flies are not needed. Best time to fish here is early spring and during wet falls.

Castle Creek Access

Access to Castle Creek is excellent in the lower few miles of the stream because Castle Crags State Park is in this section of the creek drainage. I usually fish Castle Creek from the paved road that skirts the stream on the north shore and from the Forest Service road up as far as Castle Campgrounds. After this point the road climbs away from the creek and from the South Fork of Castle Creek and access is very difficult.

Fishing Castle Creek

Castle Creek is what I call a flood plain creek, much like Shotgun and Mears creeks. The winter runoffs here have scoured the brush from the immediate area of the creek to such an extent that there is very little vegetation left near the stream itself. This makes for good fly casting because you can get a back cast of any desired size, but it also means that for most of the day the water is under full sunlight, which the trout do not like in this shallow water.

I usually fish Castle Creek during the very early morning and late evening hours. When the sun is off the water the trout are far more likely to hit than when the riffled surface is getting the full blast of the daylight sun.

The insect life in this area is much the same as it is in the other tributaries, but Castle Creek flows through rubble instead of hard rock — such as is found at Shotgun and Mears Creeks — and this means that the number of deeper holding pockets is much smaller in this creek than in the others. You have to move from one deep spot to another relatively fast to be successful with Castle Creek fishing.

I have also found that Castle Creek trout run a bit smaller on the average than the trout taken from the rest of the tributary streams. The reason is probably the lack of deeper holding water. The trout move down to the deeper waters of the Sacramento River as they reach larger sizes, seeking deeper and more protecting waters. The best bet here is to use light tackle and to move from pocket to pocket.

Soda Creek Access

Access to Soda Creek is better than it is to any of the other tributary streams to the Sacramento River. A paved county road runs right along the stream for nearly its total length and much of the time you can actually see the creek from the road.

The fact that Soda Creek is so accessible for its full length gives you a chance to fish all different types of water, from the easy flowing lower section, where shrubbery comes right down to the water's edge, to the upper sections where the creek flows through very rocky ground. Here it has a much steeper gradient that causes it to form deep pockets in a regular stairway of tiny waterfalls that provide deep pools where larger trout will be found. The gradient of the creek roughly matches that of the road and you can count on the stream to be fast flowing where the road steepens and relatively gentle flowing where

the road is flat. Usually you cannot actually see the creek from the road due to intervening growth and trees.

Fishing Soda Creek

Soda Creek is probably the most productive of all the tributary streams to the Sacramento River. It is also my own favorite among these streams. Part of this is due to the fact that access is so easy, but another thing I like about the creek is that is has such a variety of different types of water. Another thing that attracts me to this stream is that it has such a large population of different insect life that abounds in the vegetation. This insect life varies almost mile by mile as you fish upstream.

There are heavy stands of tall

Perhaps the reason that Wooly Worm flies are so effective in the Sacramento River drainage is the fact that the streamside brush is often covered with hordes of black worms like these photographed on Soda Creek in the spring.

timber and this means that it is very cool to fish Soda Creek, even during the hot summer months when fishing open waters can be such a chore. Fishing the lower stretches is much like fishing a stream in the giant redwood country on the coast. Fishing the far upper reaches is like fishing the tiny streams of the high Sierra which are virtually one continual cascade of white water.

I don't know of any section of Soda Creek where lure fishing is very productive. The few large, deep holes in the stream are so far apart that trying to work lures in these spots is not practical. However, the entire length of the stream is excellent for either bait or flies.

Nearly any bait, or baits taken right from the stream, will work, provided you use a line or leader that is light enough to suit gin clear water.

I use the same flies in Soda Creek that I use for fishing the rest of the Sacramento tributaries, except that I add a moth imitation when fishing here. During most of the season there is a heavy population of moths and other heavy wing insects that abound in the ferns and other growths along the stream. At certain times these moths make up a big part of the food found in the stomachs of Soda Creek trout and they will readily take flies like the Fan Wing Coachman or others of this type.

Lake Fishing

California is so well-endowed with trout lakes that the angler's main problem is merely to pick the right lake at the right time of year. Most of the lakes in the state are open to year-round fishing, except a few on the eastern side of the Sierra in the southern half.

The bulk of all California lake fishing takes place during the summer vacation months. Between Memorial Day and Labor Day peak utilization is reached. Probably the period between early July and mid-September is more important to trout fishermen than any other time of year. At this time of year trout fishing is about as difficult as it gets during the entire year. The reason for this is that the summer sun has warmed the surface layers of water and trout have gone deeper to escape this surface heat.

Temperature and Trout

More than any other single element water temperature controls trout habits. It can be stated as simply as: find the right temperature for trout and you'll get good fishing during the warm weather months. It makes sense to buy and use a thermometer for summer fishing.

Summer Lake Fishing

Consistent success in summer lake fishing is a matter of attention to detail. The key to good results during the hot weather months is systematic elimination of those sections that do not contain an appreciable number of trout.

Most of our lakes are deep. Just about any lake that is over 70 feet deep will stratify during warm summer weather. There will be a layer of upper water (the epilimnion) with warm water, which can be perhaps 75 degrees at the surface, generally extending down 10 to 20 feet with a temperature of about 65 degrees at the bottom. Under this layer of water is the thermocline, a relatively thin band of water, where the temperature drops about a half a degree per foot. Below this is the hypolimnion, a cold water area of around 40 degress that extends to the bottom of the lake.

Trout will move into the upper section of the lake only for brief periods when a lake is stratified. They will usually move up to feed early or late in the day, then return to more comfortable water in either the thermocline or just under it. Usually there is a lack of oxygen in the very deepest parts of a lake and trout stay away from these areas.

Complications

It would be nice to say trout can always be found in a certain section of any lake, like the thermocline, but things aren't that simple. Many things affect lakes. The size of the lake can be important to trout behavior. In very big impoundments trout can be completely absent from one section of the lake and crowded together in another. Prevailing winds that blow for several days, or for parts of most days, can pile up oxygenated water on the windward shore. This tends to cause baitfish to move to these areas. Gamefish will move with the baitfish and may be laying just off the windward shore in water deeper than the baitfish prefer.

In smaller lakes a prevailing wind can actually cause a mixing action between the warm upper layer and the thermocline. This is one reason you may find fishing very good off a point of land that juts out into the lake. As prevailing winds push water and nutrients around these points, the warmer surface gets mixed with cooler water from the depths. This causes trout to move to this section. They aren't moving to these spots so much because of the hole in the warm layer as for the concentration of baitfish and othe food they find in these areas. In effect, these are trout dining rooms. Once you find one, you've found a trout fishing bonanza.

Water Manipulation

The vast majority of our trout lakes are artificial. Various agencies have built these impoundments for the purpose of manipulating the water for irrigation, domestic water supply or power-making. This means continual raising or lowering of the water level in a lake and will cause drastic changes in the fishing.

Care in releasing will allow a trout to live and fight another day.

I have found, in general, when the water level is rising anglers usually find poor fishing. This puzzled me for years until I doped out the reason. The trout have to feed, regardless of what agencies do with the water level. I found they concentrate in the areas of the inflowing water. This is easy to see when we are dealing with a lake that gets its inflow from an open creek or flume. It is not so apparent when the inflow comes from a pipe or tunnel underwater. If the lake is rising, move to these areas to fish. Trout naturally move to these areas because there is a massive inflow of food being carried by the inflowing water.

Trout Tubes

The inflow of many lakes is natural. Only feeder streams provide this inflow but many of the outlets come from deep within the lake. Typical is a power operation where generators are located at the base of the dam or a distance downslope. As water is drawn from deep within the lake it has the effect of drawing warmer water from the upper layers and cold water from the depths and mixing them together. This is what is called a "trout tube" in many lakes.

In the case of Lake Berryessa, trout were not stocked when the lake was first formed. Biologists decided this lake, located at low elevation and fed by warm water streams, would not be suitable for trout survival. But landlocked steelhead, trapped upstream from the dam site, survived and provided the few anglers who knew about them with good fishing for several years. They could survive because the trout tube provided an area with ideal water temperature conditions for several miles back from the face of the dam.

You have probably noted that in many lakes one of the best places to fish for trout during summer months is near the dam. The trout tube effect is probably the reason.

Ask the Resorter

The visiting angler doesn't usually have time to dope out the reasons why fishing for trout is good in one area and not in another in a large impoundment. Trying to figure out if the lake has a trout tube or not is time consuming. About the best shortcut for summer fishing is simply asking local anglers, resorters or dock operators where people usually catch trout. Also, where they've been taken recently.

The resorters and dock operators want you to take fish. They know if you are successful you may come back and use their facilities. You can usually count on what they say since their business profit depends on how happy the fisherman is.

Proper Temperature

It is impossible to say that a given species of trout will always be found at exactly a certain temperature. There are too many factors involved. For instance, trout in high-elevation lakes seem to prefer water that is a couple of degrees cooler than trout in lower elevation waters.

Another factor is the various strains of trout that have been stocked in our lakes by the Department of Fish & Game. A rainbow trout that came from the kamloops rainbow strain, imported from Canada originally, seems to prefer water about five degrees cooler than most rainbow strains. If the plant came from one of the steelhead strains taken from California waters they seem to prefer water the same temperature as native rainbows. If the plant came from eggs imported from Oregon, Washington or British Columbia they want five degree colder water.

I have proved this to my own satisfaction by watching what various populations in selected lakes were doing. I use an electronic sonar device and can see the trout on the scope when they are in deep water. (See "Equipment for Trout Fishing.") Checking with a thermometer, then fishing for the trout, confirmed these findings.

The only practical advice I can give is to look for water that is between 50 and 58 degrees. I've found various thermometers can be a few degrees off. If you work with your own thermometer long enough you will find the formula that works best for your type of fishing.

The Turnovers

In the spring and again in the fall lakes go through what anglers call the turnover. This is caused by cool surface water pressing down on deeper water. At 39.2 degrees water gets as heavy as it's going to get. Any warmer or colder and water rises.

The net effect as far as the angler is concerned is that during and just after the turnover trout can be found in all sections of a lake. This is the time most anglers consider the best of the year. Trout will be found in shallow water and can be taken readily from shore or with shallow fished lures or bait.

The turnovers, or prime seasons, take place at different times of the year depending on altitude. At lower elevation lakes the prime time arrives first. Mid-elevation lakes are next and very high mountain lakes are last. An angler can use this factor to advantage. Fish the lower lakes early and late in the year and those at very high altitude during the summer and early fall months. This is a big advantage for California anglers.

Lake Techniques

It is almost always better to fish lakes from a boat. A boat gives a fisherman much more choice in the techniques he can use to take trout. The shore angler is limited to fishing only a relatively small section of water within casting distance of shore. The shore fisherman should do everything possible to mitigate this handicap.

Lake Survey

Just as in stream fishing, the lake fisherman should make a survey of conditions before he begins fishing. It is not a good idea to merely walk down to the shore and start fishing. Odds are only a few spots on any

Spinning equipment is often best in lake fishing because you can cover more water with it.

lake are really good for shore fishing. The same goes for boat fishing, only the boat fisherman can work the entire lake.

The simplest way to survey fishing at a lake is to talk to anglers who have been fishing it successfully. Try to determine where fish have been taken recently and what was used to take them. If the lake has a resort or dock ask the operators there.

A drive around the lake to various access points will often turn up some spots that are better than others. This is particularly true for shore fishermen. Undoubtedly there will be spots where shore fishermen are more successful than others.

Feeder Streams

A key spot to fish in any lake is where a feeder stream enters. Trout gather at these spots for several reasons. In the fall brown trout gather off the mouths of feeder streams, waiting for the water to rise so they can enter them to spawn. In the spring rainbows gather, getting ready for their spawning runs.

Water coming into the lake is well-oxygenated because it has been flowing. Trout become more active in oxygenated water. Since the inflow brings food with it, both baitfish and trout gather to feed. Often this water from an inflowing stream will be much cooler than the surface water of a lake, so the trout will tend to work closer to the surface near feeder streams.

Lake Outlet

Where a lake pours over a spillway is usually a good spot to fish. The siphoning action of the moving water brings food from the lake to the area near the spillway, as well as setting up currents that attract trout. If the lake is being drained, it's usually a good idea to fish near the dam, where the outlet is normally located. If the lake is drained from some other spot, such as an underwater pipe, try to determine where the pipe is located.

All lakes have currents. Some are caused by temperature change, some by winds. But the biggest currents are caused by the manipulation of water by the operators of the impoundments.

Trolling

The most popular method of taking California trout in lakes is trolling. Most anglers seem to prefer trolling with flashers, big spinners rigged with from two to six blades. When these are drawn through the water all the spinners turn at once. A keel is usually included with this kind of rig to keep the line from twisting.

Because of drag associated with the revolving spinners, flasher fishermen use heavier equipment. The spinners tend to plane lure or bait toward the surface as they move through the water. Therefore, if trout are very deep, it is necessary to use additional weights of considerable size to get down to the fish. (See "Equipment for Trout Fishing.") In extreme cases, when trout are very deep, anglers also have to use wire lines to get deep. Wire line is very bulky and anglers have to use reels more suitable to ocean fishing than those usually used for trout.

Casting near the mouths of feeder streams to lakes is always a good bet. The water is cooler here and the food is rich.

Trolling Methods

I prefer to use lines as light as possible for my own fishing. I normally rig with four-pound test monofilament on a standard fresh-water spinning reel. With this line I can get down to reasonable depths with little weight. The small diameter of four-pound test monofilament causes very little drag as it moves through the water. With an ounce or so of weight the line will go down at a very sharp angle when trolled at extremely low speed. Four-pound test is about as small as is practical for trolling; it will support a fair amount of weight and still handle larger trout well in the open waters of a lake.

Fishing a Lake

Perhaps an outline of how I go about fishing a new lake will help novice anglers. Naturally I try to find out everything I can about a lake before I launch my boat. If several other fishermen (or a resorter or dock operator) tell me all the trout are being taken in a certain place in a certain way, I head for this spot first, providing it makes sense. The only information I ignore is advice that I have to use flashers. I've never found flashers necessary and usually they are a handicap. In larger lakes it is almost essential to get some indication where fishing "should" be good. I follow this plan even though it is less important to me than to most anglers, since I have an electronic locating device. When I am surveying a lake the first day I very quickly check out the areas that I've been told are good. By placing the sending unit of the fish locator on the floor of my aluminum boat the unit will transmit and receive through the metal hull. Trout will show in the scope even when I run the boat at fairly high speeds. I can cover a great deal of water this way, while the fast-moving boat passes over even shallow-swimming fish without spooking them.

Fishing Pattern

If I don't have any particular infor-

mation about the lake, I fish in a regular pattern. I get on the water as soon as it's legal to fish. I've found that the first few hours of the day and the last few in the evening are worth more than the rest of the hours of the day put together. Trout tend to be more active during hours when the light is subdued. Also, the more hours of fishing time you've got, the better your chances of figuring out the fishing and taking trout in a given lake.

If I am fishing a small lake with a live feeder stream I immediately head for the area near it. I rig a spoon or wobbler. They are the most convenient to fish of all lure types and trout will hit them as readily as any other type. Often there are signs

Fishing near the outflow from a dam is always a good bet.

Getting set up for a day of fishing on a lake. Note the amount of tackle and the different rods being loaded here.

of fish activity. If so, the primary problem is solved: the question of whether or not there are fish to be had in the area. I begin to cast to any sign of activity. If there is no sign, I try to locate the channel of the inflowing stream.

Fish Channel

The underwater channel of an inflowing stream is a good spot for trout. They can lie in the channel, in the deepest water in the area, and move out of this protection to feed in the food-rich shallower water nearby. If they can find them, trout always prefer the edges of deeper channels and trenches to open or flat bottom water.

Often I can take several trout by fishing near the feeder stream before the sun is even on the water. If the trout are cruising this area, or actively feeding on aquatic insects, I am ready because I always take a fly rod along when I fish any lake. Although trout will hit lures when they are actively feeding on insects, they are far more likely to hit a well-presented fly that imitates the hatch they are feeding on. If you can match the hatch you are in for some exciting fishing.

It's always a good idea, even for the angler who doesn't fly fish, to bring along some flies on each trip. If you rig these on a dropper strand a few feet up the line, with the bubble on the end of the line, you can take advantage of a fly hatch when it occurs.

Shoreline Casting

If I don't catch the trout I want, or decide to continue searching for a better fishing area, I usually begin to cast along the shoreline. If there is a convenient wind blowing down the length of the shoreline, I let it move the boat. If not, I put the motor in reverse and back down the shoreline a convenient casting distance out from shore.

When trout are feeding they tend to cruise parallel to shore at a certain depth. In just about all the lakes in California you will find minnows in the shallows along shore. Trout know this and come to these areas to feed. If there are points of land jutting out into the lake I flip the motor out of gear so I can devote more time and attention to them. These are natural gathering spots and every trout cruising the shore has to cross these points, even the trout that are working fairly deep.

Methodical Trolling

If I still haven't found trout, or want to try a different technique, I begin trolling. I use the same wobbler or lure I used for casting, adding no additional weight for the first few passes. These passes are made a short distance out from shore and parallel to it. If no trout hit, I rig a dropper stand about three or four feet up the line from the lure.

Shoreline casting can be very productive when trout come in to feed on minnows.

Dropper Rigging

The simplest way to rig a dropper is to use a barrel swivel. Tie the leader to one loop; to the other, tie the dropper and the main line leading to the reel. I add perhaps a half-ounce of weight to a large snap swivel, then determine the amount of line I have out. This is done by taking the reel out of the anti-reverse setting and backing off on the reel a certain number of turns, say 30 turns to start.

If fishing has been critical I rig a dropper strand about four feet long of line lighter than the line on the reel. Then, if it gets hung up on the bottom, it can be broken off without losing an expensive lure. Another way to make the dropper strand break before the main line and leader is to tie an overhand knot in it. This will cause the line to break at about one half of its normal breaking strength. This reason for the long dropper strand is so the weight can be trolled closer and closer to shore until it begins to touch bottom occasionally. This keeps the weight and lure just off the bottom in the right place where trout cruise.

I always use a snap swivel large enough to accommodate several weights and keep adding weights until I reach a maximum for comfortable fishing. I keep track of how much weight is on at all times, as well as how much line is out. The speed of the boat is kept constant. You can check this by making a series of marks on the throttle handle and the throttle. I may change lures several times during this kind of trolling.

Depth Control

The objective in trolling is to determine what combination of line, boat speed, weight and lure is effective in that lake on that day. Normally, if you manage to take a single trout with a certain combination you can return to that depth and catch as many trout as you want. Often the combination will work for several weeks, until conditions change. If you don't know how much line is out and what weight and lure combination you were using, you can't go back to exactly the same depth to take additional trout.

On a normal day of trolling I will take at least some trout no matter what conditions are. With methodical trolling it rarely takes more than a full day to dope out the right combination. Even some seemingly small things count.

There are situations where trout hit while I am trolling into the wind and none when trolling with it. This is because the lure is running at a shallower depth with the additional speed added by a wind. Obviously, the solution is either to troll only into the wind or to let out additional line for the downwind leg of trolling.

Sometimes trout are so bunched up they hit in only a single location. Rather than continuing to troll in this kind of situation it's better to stop and cast to the spot where the fish are holding. It's a waste of time to spend trolling time out of the payoff zone.

Baitfish

Some of our larger lakes, such as

Berryessa, Shasta and Oroville, have huge populations of baitfish like threadfin shad. Even if an angler uses heavy equipment for his trolling, he should also have a lighter outfit rigged and in the boat. Often threadfins will be chased to the surface by feeding trout. Instead of trolling through the massed bait it's better to drift outside the area and cast to where the feeding is taking place. With the heavy rig this is not possible. I've even had some excel-lent days fishing these baitfish schools with flies.

Eagle Lake and Davis Lake

In most of your fishing at these two lakes you will be trying for rainbow trout and rainbows rarely are found alone. They normally run in schools and when you hook one you can be almost sure that others are in the same location.

Eagle Lake

Eagle Lake is a nearly perfect trout fishing lake. Located as it is just over the 5000 foot level, the waters of the lake remain at a good temperature for an extended period of time each year that is much longer than for lakes that are located either higher or at lower elevations. And at the 5000 foot level the weather is ideal for nearly the entire season and the fisherman here has comfortable weather for the greater part of the season.

Eagle Lake Trout

At one time the Eagle Lake trout was nearly extinct. This is a very critical thing because the Eagle Lake trout is unique. It is the only type of trout that can stand the very high alkaline content found in Eagle Lake. Transplants of other kinds of trout have always failed. The Department of Fish & Game has made a remarkable and successful attempt to bring back trout fishing at Eagle Lake. They set up an egg taking sta-tion on the major feeder stream, Pine Creek, and they take all of the eggs from these fish and then raise them artificially until the trout are of catchable size. They then release the trout into Eagle Lake and the present population of these unique trout runs at a high level.

Trout Size

At Eagle Lake you will find that the available trout will generally run to specific sizes, dependant on which of the Fish & Game plants the individual trout have come from. Normally the trout in the average stringer will run from 1 to 1½ pounds in one class, 2 to 2½ pounds in another class and 3 to 8 pounds for the larger trout that have successfully lived through several years of growth. And the growth rate at Eagle Lake for these trout is outstanding. The Eagle Lake trout are deep bodied and the flesh is both firm and fine grained, making them some of the finest eating trout in the world.

Early in the morning and late in the evenings you can take a limit of Eagle Lake trout wading and fishing off the edges of the grass beds. This area can also be worked from a boat by casting inshore to the edges of the grass.

The limit on Eagle Lake is three fish per day and three fish in possession. This may seem like a small number of trout to try for, but when you consider the fact that you will rarely take small trout at any time and that you can try for larger individual specimens that actually are trophy class fish in any fishery, the three fish per day limit is not what could be considered unreasonable.

Trout Habits

In general Eagle Lake trout habits are the same as those for the rain-bow species wherever they are found. However, there are some specific things about Eagle Lake trout and Eagle Lake trout fish-ing that are unique enough for comment.

Eagle Lake is basically a spring fed lake. It does have a few small feeder streams, the largest of which is Pinc Crcek. But even Pine Creek is a very small stream when compared with the streams that feed most lakes. And, being spring fed, due to the fact that the surrounding coun-try is mostly lava rock grounds, the cooler water during the summer months will be found at or near these springs.

Underwater Springs

I feel sure that there must be hundreds, if not thousands, of underwater springs at Eagle Lake. I have located only a few for my own fishing and they are marked on the map included here. An angler can locate these springs by merely using a common fishing thermometer during the warm water months of summer and early fall. Finding these springs and locating them exactly is a time consuming thing because the temperature variation is small even during the hot summer months, but this can be critical to successful fishing, especially during the middle of the day when the larger trout retreat to these spring areas to find cool water. But the effort is worth it to locate these cool water areas because nearly all the worthwhile trout will be there.

Gallatin Spring

One of the largest spring areas is located off Gallatin Beach. This is a favorite area for summer fishermen. Most of the fishing here is done with bait fished right off the bottom. To locate this important spring look for a water tank on the east shore on the flank of the mountain. The springs are located nearly due west and a few hundred feet out from this shore.

Pikes Spring

A very large spring is located on the edge of a deep channel that runs north and south from Pikes Bay to Wildcat Point. There is a vast amount of water here and this spring area is hard to find but it can be located approximately by sighting a line from the marina to the camp at Circus Grounds and another from Wildcat Point to Pikes Bay. At ice out time this spring can be pinpointed because the ice goes out here first.

Bucks Springs

The springs marked on either side of Bucks Point are very important for anglers fishing the north end of Eagle Lake because this entire end of the lake is relatively shallow and during warm weather this area becomes a warm water zone. The trout will either leave this area completely or they will bunch up at these underwater springs.

Locating Springs

The exact location of underwater springs and seeps of cold water can be all important to the angler fishing Eagle Lake during the hot months of July, August and September. At this time of year, when the relatively shallow waters of Eagle Lake warm up to a great extent, most of the worthwhile trout in the lake will congregate in the areas near the cool, comfortable water of these springs.

When it comes to locating springs such as the large ones on shore at Gallatin Beach all the angler has to do is to look along the shoreline where he can usually spot small groves of aspens that grow where these springs are flowing. But when it comes to locating the exact spot where the underwater springs enter the lake the angler has no visual indication as to the exact

Eagle Lake

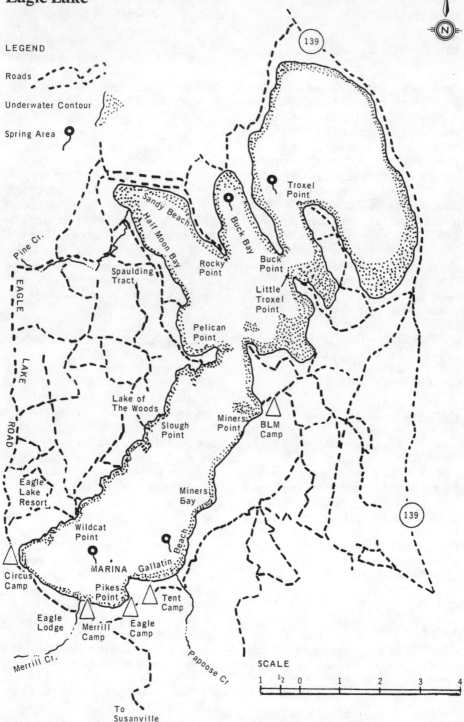

LEGEND

Roads

Underwater Contour

Spring Area

SCALE

spot where these springs are located. The only answer to this problem for the serious fisherman is to utilize a fishing thermometer.

Fishing Thermometer

Because temperature is the most critical element in the habitat of trout and other fish, we always recommend that a good fishing thermometer be used.

It is not enough for the Eagle Lake fisherman to own a good fishing thermometer, the devices must be used correctly. In my own fishing I use two thermometers. One thermometer is hooked to the fish stringer right at the surface and hung over the side of the boat. I have found that often a wind or wave action will homogenize the water in a lake like Eagle Lake and cause cool waters to rise from the depths to cool the surface. Too, the thermometer hooked to the stringer can tell the angler a lot about his own fishing methods and it is very easy to check the thermometer right next to the boat.

When surface temperatures are up in the high 60's and 70's there is little chance that trout will be in shallow water. The only time that trout will enter this zone is early and late in the day when they come into the shallows to feed. And when the surface temperature of the water is very much over the 65 degree level the angler should begin to try to find an underwater spring or some other source of cold water.

To locate hidden springs the thermometer is simply hooked to the line, using the same snap swivel as is used for hooking a lure to the fishing line. The thermometer is then cast out in the same way that a plug or other lure is cast and allowed to settle to the bottom. It must rest there for a minute or two before it is retrieved so that the water in the barrel of the thermometer has a chance to cool to the temperature on the bottom. Then it is retrieved fast and read immediately.

Right Temperature

I have found that a difference of 5 to 8 degrees usually occurs in areas near the springs at Eagle Lake and when you find an area that is this much cooler than the general temperature of the lake you can be sure that you have located a spring that flows into the bottom of the lake. You can also be sure that virtually all of the better fish will be holding in this temperature zone.

The perfect temperature for Eagle Lake trout is around 58 degrees. This does not mean that you have to locate this exact temperature in order to take trout. Instead, you are trying to find temperatures as near to the 58 degree level as possible. The important thing is to locate an area with a large enough variation in temperature, on the cooler side, than in the surrounding water.

Eagle Lake Access

There is a very good launching ramp located at the marina just west of Gallatin Beach where larger boats can be put in the water. The cartop boat can be put into the water at just about any point on the lake, but the shoreline nearly everywhere is very shallow and weed filled, so using waders is usually necessary to get enough water under the boat to run the prop.

Eagle Lake regulars get used to this type of berthing and launching and you will see literally hundred of boats pulled up along the shores near the camps.

Eagle Lake Camps

At Eagle Lake camping has become an art. The Forest Service has some large campgrounds at the south end of the lake that are among the finest I have ever seen. At the Circus Grounds there are rough sites used by anglers who bring their trailers and tents and leave them for the entire season. This area is slated for another Forest Service campground when money for it becomes available. I feel that this would mean that the regulars who come every week to enjoy the lake will simply have to move still one more time. The Forest Service has been chasing the Circus Ground people all along the shores and it would probably be a good idea for them to admit that these people at the Circus Grounds should have at least one area where they can leave their trailers and gear.

There are Bureau of Land Management campsites and many rough campsites at nearly any spot where there is an access road to the lake. I suggest that anyone wanting to place a trailer at the end of one of these roads check out the road before they decide to try. In this lava rock country the roads are usually very rough.

A fine double limit of Eagle Lake trout taken casting along shore to the grass beds near Pelican Point. The trout hold near these grass beds waiting for a meal of Tui Chub minnows. Early or late in the day is the best time.

Eagle Lake Trolling

The majority of anglers who fish Eagle Lake do their fishing by trolling and many trout are taken this way. Wobblers and plugs such as the Rebel are the favorite lures for this kind of trolling. Most anglers merely tie the lure on the end of the line and then troll at a fairly good clip. But adding some weight to the line above the lure is certainly much better than merely using the lure alone. By tying on a swivel 3 to 5 ft. above the lure the angler can then make a dropper strand and by varying the amount of weight he can fish the lures at different depths.

I personally do not consider trolling as a particularly good method of fishing Eagle Lake. I have found that on most days of trolling I am lucky to show with even a three fish limit. Eagle Lake is about 15 miles long and 5 miles wide on the average and unless you are trolling in exactly the right depth, the trolling cannot be very productive. At Eagle Lake I use the trolling technique only as a last resort.

Fish Shallows

As we have pointed out, the trout will go into the shallows near the drowned weed beds when they get ready to feed. In order to prove this all the angler need do is to cruise along the shoreline a few feet out from the weed beds and watch as trout scoot out from under the boat.

In the spring and fall when the waters of Eagle Lake are cooled to around the 55 to 60 degree level the trout will even be in these shallows during the middle of the day. At around the 58 degree surface temperature level I have even found that the trout will usually not come into the shallows to feed until about mid-morning, then they'll stay almost all day. Of course, in the spring the minnows are not as numerous as they are later in the year and the trout have to wait longer in order to catch enough of them to satisfy their appetites. In the summer and early fall the minnows are so thick that the trout can find enough feed in a short time. Once they have fed they generally retreat to deeper water to spend the balance of the day. I have confirmed this with my Fish Lokator and have found that most of the trout will be at around 40 to 45 feet in deeper channels where they can find cooler waters.

The angler really should take the time out to check these facts out for his own fishing. The idea of merely cruising the shoreline where the water is clear will prove that the bulk of the trout are in these areas. It is very difficult to troll effectively in the areas very near the weed beds because the angler who trolls here will spend too much time taking moss and weeds off his lures. Casting spoons, plugs or even bait as the boat moves along in these shallow areas is the top technique for taking Eagle Lake trout. The only difference is that during the warm water months the trout will generally be in these areas early and late in the day and in the cool months they will be in these areas at nearly any time of the day.

Shore Fishing

Almost every year, at the beginning of the season, anglers who fish from shore do better than those fishing from boats. The reasons are ex-

Trolling is the best method of locating the places in lakes that the trout prefer. The angler should generally then stop trolling and cast to the fish. It is a good idea to have more than one outfit, each rigged with different line.

plained above. But the shore fisherman will find that he will do much better if he fishes in fairly close to shore in areas 5 to 8 feet in depth rather than to cast very far out into the deeper water. There will be trout in the deeper offshore areas but for every one that lays off in deeper water there will be many more that move in close.

The shore fisherman will also find that his scores will go up if he moves around. Eagle Lake trout have the habit of moving into the shoreline area and then staying in a very limited area. This is a strange habit for rainbow trout because normally the species will come inshore and then cruise along the shoreline as they feed. But the Eagle Lake strain seems to have this habit of taking up a stand in one spot after reaching the inshore

area. I think the reason for this is that the fish in Eagle Lake are so large as individuals they have developed solitary feeding habits. So the shore fisherman who moves along the bank instead of just fishing a single spot has a lot better chance of offering his baits or lures to a larger number of trout than the angler who stays in one spot.

In areas where the shore tapers off gradually it is even possible to wade and cast to the trout at the outside of the weed beds. The trout rarely actually enter the thicker weed beds but they lie just off the edges and it is necessary to wade fairly deep in order to reach them. If you try to stay on dry land and fish these areas you'll find that it is almost impossible to keep the weeds off the lure or bait when they are retrieved.

Returning to Spots

The angler who fishes Eagle Lake very much will soon find that certain areas of the lake are far more productive than other areas. The reasons for this are that either there is a cool spring in certain areas or that there is a sharp underwater dropoff or even a deep lava rock trench in these areas where the trout can find cooler water at these greater depths. These things are self evident for the angler who has a fish locating device, but the majority of fishermen do not own an electronic depth device and having the ability to return to an area that is productive can be critical to fishing success. In fact, I've never found another lake where fishing success depended so much on being able to pinpoint the exact location of good fishing spots as at Eagle Lake.

The method used by anglers to return to exact spots on a lake is called triangulation. This is a fancy word for simply lining up objects on shore in two different directions so that when you sight an imaginary line between them you have a straight line. Then by turning a 90 degree angle and sighting two other objects on other shores, the fisherman can line up the spot within a very few feet. In Eagle Lake with perhaps 75 square miles of water to be fished this art is important.

Eagle Lake Flies

I have checked the stomach contents of several dozen Eagle Lake trout and have found a lot of insect

By cutting open the stomachs of these Eagle Lake trout it could be determined that a small scud or freshwater shrimp was the main item on their diet during the spring months. The trout also contained a great number of pale mayflies.

Streamer flies can be trolled effectively for Eagle Lake trout. This streamer and other larger patterns do a good job of imitating the Tui Chub minnows, which are a major item on the menu for Eagle Lake rainbows.

food in them. During the spring and summer, and any time until the first really heavy freezes of fall, the Eagle Lake trout have a large number of small flies that look like a pale evening mayfly. I have checked several books on these flies and cannot find the specific fly that these fish eat. However, an Adams fly in about size No. 14 comes close to imitating these Eagle Lake flies.

Biologists tell me that the same high alkalinity content of Eagle Lake that makes the lake livable to only the Eagle Lake trout and the Tui Chub also means a great many changes in the insect content of the lake. This means that the trout are very selective in their feeding and they will not normally hit the same flies that are productive in other bodies of fresh water.

I have never personally had much luck with dry flies at Eagle Lake. In a few cases I have taken a limited number of trout on gaudy patterns such as the McGinty and Royal Coachman patterns, but these times are relatively rare. A much better bet is to fish with bucktails and streamers in the shallows.

You can get some eye popping sport fishing just over or near the weed beds that line sections of the shoreline at Eagle Lake. This is particularly true early and late in the day when the larger fish come into the shallows to feed on the hordes of small fish that hide in the weeds. In most sections it is difficult to fish these weed beds from the shore and it is best done from a boat either anchored or drifting some distance from the weed beds. I have watched on my Fish Lokator in the mornings and evenings as literally hundreds and even thousands of bigger fish move inshore just at dusk and at sunrise to feed on the minnows. This is why fishing with minnow imitations is so productive. You only have to sink the flies to 5 or 10 feet on most days.

Eagle Lake Shrimp

I have never cut open the stomach of an Eagle Lake trout and failed to find a large selection of pale pink shrimps. These shrimps, probably fresh water scuds, are about five eighths of an inch long and they can be imitated almost exactly with a Horner Shrimp pattern tied on a No. 10 hook. The offering certainly is valid enough if the angler can dope out the correct time and place to fish this way.

Eagle Lake trout also have had a lot of small shells in them when I've checked their stomachs. And a surprising number of them have lava rocks of various sizes. They evidently ingest these rocks when they are grubbing the bottom for either the shrimp or shells.

Tui Chub

I feel that the primary offering of Eagle Lake trout should be the minnow imitations of the Tui Chub minnows that you will see by the millions in the grass beds that line the lake. I have found that early and late in the day the trout will lie right off the edges of these grass beds and feed on these massed schools of minnows. And, even though they will eat scuds, mayflies and other items, the larger specimens seem to prefer the big mouthful that these chub minnows provide.

Sometimes the angler will hook and land the larger Tui Chubs. In fact, the chubs are sometimes so numerous that it is necessary to

Eagle Lake trout are a special breed and they have outstanding fighting and eating qualities. The fish generally run an average of around 2 pounds throughout the year, but there are many individual fish that will scale over the 5 or 6 pound mark.

Some flies that work well at Eagle Lake. Note that these flies are relatively large (compare with quarter). In general, the bigger trout seem to want flies of larger size that make the effort of chasing them worth it.

move to another spot because they will not let a lure or fly alone long enough for the trout to take the offering. I have heard several anglers say that these chubs are good to eat, but I cannot confirm this fact. With the Eagle Lake trout rated as one of the finest eating trout in the world I've never bothered to try the Tui Chub on my own plate.

Davis Lake

Davis Lake, much like Eagle Lake, is a nearly perfect trout fishing lake. When it is full the surface of the lake stands at the 5775 ft. level which is about the ideal altitude for producing trout fishing at its best. At this elevation the seasons run for a longer period of time than they do at either higher elevations—where the seasons are short—or at lower elevations—where the water warms too fast and the trout go too deep for good fishing.

Like Eagle Lake, Davis Lake is a comparatively shallow body of water. This means that the sun can penetrate to good depths in these wide expanses of open water and generate a good deal of aquatic vegetation, which promotes the growth of aquatic insect life. As the water rises in the spring to the spillway height of 5775 ft. this flooding causes an explosion in this underwater growth factor to a remarkable degree. As the water level drops through the summer and fall months the shallower depths are penetrated by the sun on a continual basis. These factors combine to make Davis one of the most prolific waters in California when it comes to trout food.

Davis Lake Record

Since Davis Lake was opened to the public it has produced an amazing quantity of fish of good size for an almost endless number of anglers. For a lake of only a 4000 acre surface area Davis Lake has supported up to 20,000 man days of fishing pressure on a single day. An average

of 10,000 to 15,000 visitation days has been recorded during the 1970 season, according to the Forest Service. And still, the majority of anglers end up taking trout. This is a record that is very difficult to top in any body of water no matter where it is located.

In past seasons Davis Lake has been the wonder of trout fishing in California. Unlike most trout lakes, Davis Lake continues to provide high quality trout fishing through the entire season, right up until the closing months. Even during summer an angler can expect to take trout at Davis Lake if he is willing to fish properly. The trout may come a

Shore fishermen take plenty of Davis Lake trout. Fishing near the tributary streams is preferred, but these anglers fished for limits near a dry tributary on the north shore. Winter runoff has scoured out a deep hole in this area.

Davis Lake

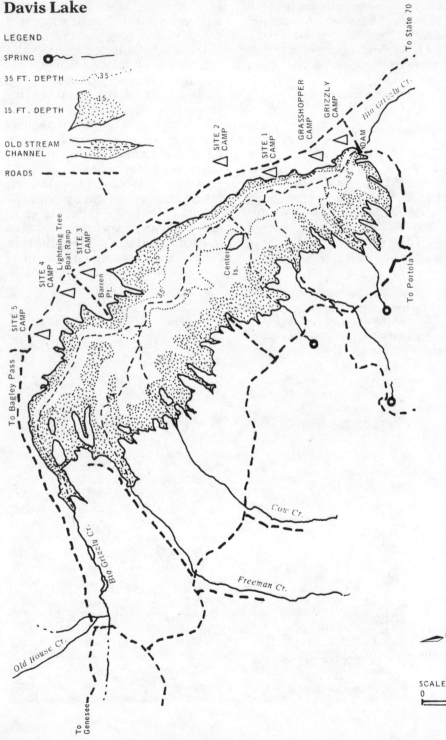

LEGEND

SPRING

35 FT. DEPTH   ·····35·····

15 FT. DEPTH

OLD STREAM
CHANNEL

ROADS

SITE 2
CAMP

SITE 1
CAMP

GRASSHOPPER
CAMP

GRIZZLY
CAMP

To State 70

Big Grizzly Cr.

DAM

To Portola

Lightning Tree
Boat Ramp

SITE 3
CAMP

SITE 4
CAMP

SITE 5
CAMP

Barren
Pt.

Center
Is.

To Bagley Pass

Big Grizzly Cr.

Old House Cr.

To
Genesee

Cow Cr.

Freeman Cr.

SCALE
0   1/2

bit harder during the hot months of August and September but an angler willing to fish can still take a reasonable number of them by fishing early and late in the day.

Trout Size

Through the season I have found that the optimum trout taken from Davis Lake will run 1 to 1½ pounds in the take for an average day of fishing. The trout vary in size according to the class of Department of F&G plantings that they come from. Trout that are a year or two old will generally run from 2 to 2½ pounds and a few individual trout that have weathered several years in the lake will top the 3 and 4 pound mark.

In an average day of fishing I usually expect to take 2 or perhaps 3 trout of over 2½ pounds. This doesn't mean I can count on trout of this size, but over past seasons I have averaged trout of this size with at least a few a day showing in the creel during all months of the season. Naturally, the larger trout tend to be found deeper than smaller trout. I always release any trout of less than a pound at Davis Lake because I am certain that I can take trout of larger size.

Mayfly Hatches

I have seen more and larger mayfly hatches at Davis Lake, over a more protracted period of time, than I have ever seen at any other lake in California. For all intents there is a mayfly hatch going on almost continually in one part of the lake or another during any time from about 8 o'clock in the morning to sundown.

I feel that this is caused by the sun warming the waters over the vast stretches of the shallows as it progresses through the day. Mayfly hatches are triggered by the heat and rays of the sun and the fact that Davis has these vast shallow areas accounts for the continual ideal hatching conditions.

There are several spring fed seeps and streams that enter Davis Lake from the south and southwest. These cold springs and streams pour a continual flow of cooling water that slowly heats up when it stands in the lake. The mayflies in this section of the lake tend to hatch later in the season than those at the north and east ends of the lake. And this cold flow of water accounts for the fact that ideal hatching conditions continue throughout the season, while the shallow areas that do not have cold inflows of water provide ideal conditions for the early season months.

Some of these mayfly hatches last for a matter of hours and some take only about a half hour to run their course. It is important to realize that the stage of the hatch in progress controls the way the trout feed.

When the hatch is beginning the mayflies will be coming from the bottom to the top of the water in their nymph form. The trout begin feeding on them as they rise toward the surface. And generally you can tell if the trout are feeding on the nymph forms because they do not make a splashy rise. Instead, you may see just their heads or tails as they take the rising nymphs. But when the trout are rising to flies resting and drying on the surface you can see them sort of sipping in the insects as they float on the surface. At this time dry flies work best.

Davis Lake is noted for the high growth factor of the fish in the lake. Note how deep bodied these rainbows are for their overall length. The fact that Davis is relatively shallow and the sun penetration is good accounts for this.

Fishing the Hatches

The reason that it is so important to determine the state of the hatch is that when the trout are feeding on the nymph form of the flies they will almost all ignore any of the floating insects on the surface. But when they begin feeding actively on the floating flies they will almost all ignore the remaining nymphs that are still coming to the surface.

Often, however, as when there is a fair breeze blowing, it is impossible to determine what stage of the hatch is in progress. In this situation I merely assume that the trout are feeding on the nymph form and tie on a sinking fly. I like to use flies that have been weighted for this fishing because it takes less time for weighted nymphs to sink to the proper depth that for unweighted flies. I also generally will use a floating line for this fishing because I want to be able to change over quickly to floating flies when the trout come to the surface to feed.

It is not necessary to sink the fly clear to the bottom to take trout during the nymph stage of their feeding, but the nymph fly should be sunk as deeply as possible before it is retrieved very slowly to the surface. It is generally necessary to anchor the boat for this kind of fishing. Even the slightest breeze will carry you along at such a pace that the nymph never has a chance to sink more that a foot or two. Some anglers even insist on anchoring the boat fore and aft so that it doesn't swing on the end of a single rope. I agree that it is better to have the additional stability of two anchors but I seldom go to this much trouble in anchoring because I want to be ready to move the boat quickly and hauling up two anchors is just too much trouble.

I have had my best luck at Davis Lake using nymphs tied on small hooks. A No. 14 hook is probably the best all around size to use for Davis Lake fishing, but I like to have nymphs tied on No. 16 and No. 18 size hooks as well. The mayflies that hatch at the 6000 foot level are nearly always of the smaller variety due to the altitude and Davis Lake mayflies follow this rule in general. However, you can usually tell by watching the floating mayflies, whether the current hatch is large or small. A nymph form approximately the size of the floating insect is then in order.

Dry Flies

It is relatively simple to match a hatch of insects that you can see coming off the water so there is little need to go into this point. Most of the flies that I use for dry fishing at Davis Lake are in sizes No. 14 and No. 16 and I consider the size of the fly far more important than matching the exact color of these emerging mayflies or other insect forms. Too, I like my flies to stand up on stiff hackles. It is usually important to jiggle the fly on the surface in order to attract the attention of the busily feeding trout. Mayflies make quite a disturbance when they are shucking their nymphal skin and this is what attracts the trout into feeding. Remember, you are

This is a closeup of a two-feather fly used to imitate one of the mayfly hatches that make Davis Lake famous. The flies should come as close as possible to the emerging insects in any lake fishing because the trout have plenty of time to inspect the offering.

competing with literally thousands of natural insects that are lying on the surface already. Making a slight disturbance to imitate a nymph emerging from his nymph husk always seems to help.

Flies in Spinning

The spin fisherman should consider fishing with flies in Davis Lake. If the spin line is rigged correctly these outfits can be just as effective as fly fishing equipment, and in windy conditions the spinning outfit is often better because wind does not effect the thin line used on spinning gear as much as it does the thick fly line.

For fishing flies with spinning equipment I recommend using plastic bubbles. The type of bubble to choose is one that can be filled with either water or shot so that it will sink and can also be emptied out so that it will float. This way the same bubble can be used for both nymph or sinking flies and for floating flies as well. There is no need to use weighted sinking flies. The bubble tows the fly to the bottom.

The proper way to rig a spin line for fly fishing is to tie the bubble on the end of the line and tie the fly on a dropper strand some distance up the line from the bubble. Davis Lake is not really an extremely clear body of water but the water is generally clear enough that the leader dropper strands should be made of

Pat Freeman with the results of a morning's trout fishing at Davis Lake. These trout were taken off a point of land as they cruised the shore in search of food. On calm mornings you can see them rise as they move along the shoreline.

material of around 2 lb. test monofilament. Also, I think it is best to tie
the fly on at least 3 to 5 ft. up the line
from the bubble in order to get the
bubble out of the trout's cone of
vision.

A couple of older fishermen
tipped me to a trick that has added
many fish to my own stringer by
combining flies with spin fishing
equipment. These men rig with a
regular trout fishing lure like a
Rebel and then they tie on a fly
about 4 ft. up the line from the lure.
They use an 18 inch dropper strand
of about 2 lb. test monofilament for
the main line. When they are fishing
nymphs they use sinking flies that
are weighted and for dry fly fishing
they use a high floating fly like a Bivisible. The combination is very
effective because the lure does
everything that the floating bubble
does and the lure is often hit by larger fish. In fact, on many occasions
I've had trout nudge the floating
bubble in my own fishing and adding the lure merely gives you that
much more to offer the trout.

Davis Lake Trolling

One of the most effective ways to
take Davis Lake trout is trolling.
Generally, trolling nearly anywhere
in the lake will produce trout during the prime peak parts of the season, but when the surface waters
become warm certain spots will be
more productive than others.

On the map included with this
guide you will see that we have indicated the 15 ft. depth and the 35 ft.
depth so that the angler will have
some idea of what kind of bottom
structure is under the boat no matter where he fishes. These figures
for depth are accurate only when

the lake is at the spillway height of
5775. They indicate elevations of
5760 and 5740. However, by noting
the current depth of the lake as
against the high water mark, plainly
visible along the shoreline, the angler using this map can accurately
determine the depth in each area of
the lake.

After the spring season trout
will usually seek out water that has
a combination of shallow areas located near deep areas. The reason is
that the deeper water is cooler and
the shallower areas have much
more food in them. At least twice a
day the larger trout will move onto
the shallower areas to feed. This
normally occurs early and late in
the day during late July, August and
September. In May and again in October the trout will be found in the
shallows nearly any time of the day.

In general the top spots to troll
are located along the area marked
for 35 ft. depths. The area along the
northeast shore provides a steep
dropoff that is very easy to locate
for the troller. Another key trolling
area is at the south end of the lake
just west and north of the dam site.
Here you will note that the underwater structure of the lake at the 15
ft. depth is formed by a series of
long fingers of land under the surface. By trolling alternately north
and then south the angler can be
certain that he is trolling over this
series of underwater ridges. The
trout here lie in the deeper sections
that slope off into the 35 ft. depths
and then into still deeper water. By
trolling here you get a chance to
offer your lure or bait to the trout at
several different depths.

On the map we have indicated
the old stream beds for the major
streams that feed the lake. These

spots are generally the deepest parts of the lake and when trolling at the north end of the lake the trout are far more likely to be found in these deep sections through the warmer parts of the season than they are out on the flats of the shallow water sections. A trolling pattern that cuts across these deeper water areas is more logical than merely trolling at random in this part of the lake.

Trolling Gear

There are two schools of thought when it comes to trolling gear used at Davis and Eagle lakes. One group uses very heavy tackle that can be used for fishing very deep. The other group of anglers uses very light equipment that, when it is used with modest size weights, can be trolled at reasonably deep levels. At both lakes the trout tend to go deep, up to 50 to 60 feet, during the hot summer months. This is particularly true of the larger trout found in both lakes.

Davis Lake Feeder Streams

There are three major feeder streams noted on the map: Big Grizzly Creek, Freeman Creek and Cow Creek. These spring fed creeks all supply a constant flow of ice cold water to Davis Lake and this means

A weight limit of trout like these can be taken relatively fast once the angler determines where in the lake or stream the trout are holding. These Davis Lake rainbows were taken near the clear, cold feeder streams where they gather.

that they are gathering spots for concentrations of trout, especially in the spring and through the warm summer months.

I have never failed to find concentrations of trout near these feeder streams, particularly in the case of Freeman and Cow creeks. At the spot where the cold water from the creeks mixes with the warmer water of the lake the trout find nearly perfect conditions. They can relax in the cool water and be close to the food-rich but warmer shallow water of the lake. They will generally be found in depths of around 15 to 20 ft. except when they are feeding. When they move up into shallower water you can actually see them when there is no wind blowing across the water. Some of the most exciting fishing I have ever done is early morning and late evening fishing near these feeders. At this time of day the trout are feeding actively and you can often see them moving around. The excitement comes from spotting a fish and then casting directly in the path of his movement. If you cast directly to the trout it will usually spook him. For this fishing I generally use a Wooly Worm fly unless there is a hatch coming off and the trout are actively feeding on it.

Davis Lake Flies

Davis Lake is an excellent fly fishing lake. I can't remember a single time that I've fished the lake that there weren't several good hatches during each day. For lake fishing in Davis I use lightly hackled flies when the surface is calm and patterns such as the Gordon, Dark and Light Cahill, Black Gnat, Adams and Hendrickson will get the job done. More important than the patterns here is the size of the fly used. I use flies in No. 16 to No. 12 and have even gone to size No. 20 on occasion at Davis Lake.

When the winds blow and hatches occur I use Bivisibles and Wulff patterns. The deer hair patterns are also good in choppy water.

Streamer and bucktail patterns can produce some stimulating fishing at Davis Lake. You can choose just about any point of land that juts out into the lake and be almost assured that these streamers and bucktails will produce early and late. The trout cruise the shoreline at this time of day and they usually come close into shore near these points. The important thing is to sink the streamers and bucktails down to at least 10 or 15 feet deep before retrieving them.

Barren Point

The long finger of land that projects out into the lake just south and east of the boat launching site at Lightening Tree has always produced well for me. I have named and marked this area as Barren Point on the map in order to denote it as a special spot. By checking the map included with this guide you will see that a ridge of land under the water tapers off quickly into the 15 ft. depth almost directly out from this jutting point of land and trout will usually navigate this area at around the 15 ft. depth when they are moving inshore to feed.

Fishing Barren Point early and late in the day is a good idea even if the angler is fishing from a boat. I have had many good mornings and evenings of fishing here. When the wind is calm you can cast to individ-

132 - CALIFORNIA TROUT

ual fish here as they move past the point. Also, the big bay of shallow water just to the south and east of Barren Point is very productive during the summer months when the trout move into this area to feed.

Fishing Barren Point

Trout in Davis Lake do a lot of cruising when they are feeding. On calm mornings you can actually see them surfacing at regular intervals as they move progressively down the shoreline. In general these trout will stay along the 15 to 35 ft. depths as they move along parallel to the shoreline and the angler can use the map included with this guide to put himself in the right area for fishing for these trout as they cruise the shoreline.

An angler who is fishing from shore will note that only in a few spots does the 15 or 35 ft. depth come within reasonable casting distance of the shoreline. These few spots are key areas for the shore fisherman and an angler who chooses these few areas will have a much better chance of success with larger trout than the fisherman who merely fishes from a location that does not have shore access to deeper water.

Center Island

Note on the map that some very deep water can be found near Center Island where the 35 ft. depths bend in to almost touch the island at the northeast and southeast ends of the island. Anglers have found that fishing around this island is effective and you can generally see many boats anchored at random around it. The reason that fishing here is effective is the fact that the water deepens in these two spots at a rapid rate, giving the trout the sanctuary of deep water very close to shallow areas that contain a good food supply.

North Sierra Trout Fishing

The lakes and streams in California that offer premium trout fishing are found generally north of Interstate 80 and the Feather River drainage. The waters described in this section were selected mainly because they are productive. Any trout fishing trip is better when you manage to catch trout. I have bypassed waters in these same areas that didn't measure up to the quality of those included.

The Season

In general, the fishing season on these waters is determined by weather conditions. The trout-fishing season—May through mid-November in the high Sierra—corresponds generally to the time when the waters and their access are free of snow and ice. The Feather River has a special, delayed opening, and you should check the angling regulations to determine when the season opens. (No attempt was made in this guide to cover ice fishing; both the treacherous weather and difficult access make the frozen lakes largely impractical and perhaps dangerous for most fishermen.)

Of course, in the very high mountains, the trout fishing is determined entirely by weather conditions, rather than by a date in the Fish & Game regulations. Some years, the ice remains on some of these waters until June. Other years, early fall storms will keep anglers away from the waters well before the official end of the season. Even during the middle of summer, the angler should be prepared for heavy thunderstorms and sudden and unseasonal changes in the weather. Anglers should always be ready to move out of a wilderness area in a hurry if a big weather front moves in.

Fishing Conditions

I have tried to mix the types of water included in this section. Each stream should deliver good numbers of trout for the careful fisherman, although in the smaller streams in this section, you can hardly expect to take 24-inch trout.

The angler who rates his fishing success for a day on the water by the size of the trout taken should stick to larger waters, such as the dam reservoirs or big streams like the Truckee. In the Truckee you can hope to take trout of over 20 inches, and most of the larger reservoirs have been stocked with various strains of plump trout.

I personally don't rate fishing success by size alone. To me, taking a 10- to 12-inch trout from a small creek is just as big an event as taking a pot-bellied trout from larger waters. Successfully slickering a lure or bait in under trailing brush on a tiny stream can be just as satisfying as catching a weight limit of fish. Quality trout fishing is a state of mind, not a heavy stringer.

The best trout found in all these waters is the rainbow. Brown trout and remnants of other species are also available in most of these streams and lakes, but you'll find a ratio of 9 to 1 rainbows over browns in the average string.

How to Use the Maps

This section includes maps covering the lakes and streams discussed. These maps are sketched simplifications of Forest Service or other government maps. Roads and road systems that do not lead to significant fishing water were excluded. Anglers who are interested in maps with more detail can get them free from the Forest Service in the area being fished.

In wet weather, some of the roads noted on the maps are impassable. Particularly in the case of very high-altitude areas, the angler should definitely check with local authorities to determine road and travel conditions.

All of the lakes and streams in this guide are located mostly on Forest Service property, and most of the camping facilities in all the areas outlined in this section are maintained by the Forest Service. The official Forest Service maps are important for anglers mainly because they show property ownership in each area. The areas shaded green on the maps belong to the

Anglers get rigged up for a morning of stream trout fishing. Note wading staff standing against pickup. This is equipment the modern fly fisherman needs to be consistently successful.

public and are for public use. No attempt was made in this guide to show public ownership because it is continually changing.

If you want to get maps in advance of a trip to these areas, you can write to U.S. Forest Service, 630 Sansome Street, San Francisco, CA 94111. For maps to the north Tahoe and Truckee River area, ask for the Truckee District, Forest Hill, Big Bend District, and Tahoe National Forest maps. For maps of the north fork of the Feather River, ask for the Mineral District, Almanor District, Eagle Lake District, and the Quincy and Greenville District maps. Ask specifically if maps that show Forest Service ownership are available.

Fishing Methods

The reservoirs chosen for this North Sierra section are virtually all fishable both from a boat or from the shore, but a boat will definitely put you at an advantage. The boat fisherman can work the deeper sections of the lakes and can therefore go after the trout for a much longer part of the season.

In shore fishing, the best results will naturally come early in the season and then again late in the year. If the trout fisherman is free only during the vacation months, when the weather is warm, he would do best to choose the cool lakes and streams located at the

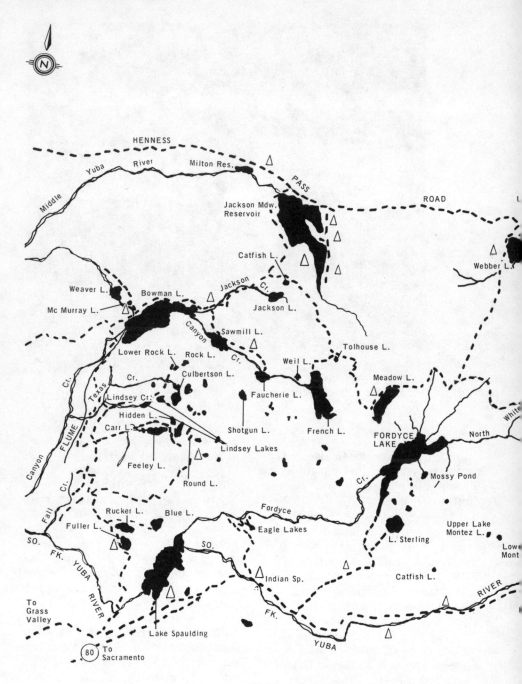

North Sierra Region

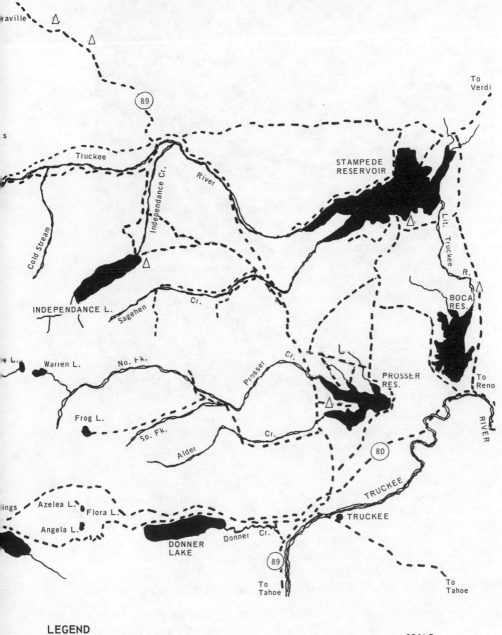

STAMPEDE
RESERVOIR

To
Verdi

Truckee

Independance Cr.

River

Lit. Truckee R.

Cold Stream

BOCA
RES.

INDEPENDANCE L.

Sagehen

Cr.

e L.

Warren L.

No. Fk.

Prosser

Cr.

PROSSER
RES.

To
Reno

RIVER

Frog L.

So. Fk.

Alder

Cr.

80

TRUCKEE

ings

Azelea L.

Flora L.

TRUCKEE

Angela L.

Donner

Cr.

DONNER
LAKE

89

To
Tahoe

To
Tahoe

LEGEND

ROADS

SCALE

1   ½ 0   1   2

Fishing can be a family sport. In summer, lakes like Prosser and Stampede have their shores lined with small boats. A speed limit makes for pleasant fishing.

highest elevations. Most of the waters in this section are located at or over 5,000 feet, where you'll find the best potential in California trout fishing regardless of when and how you fish.

The lakes in this section do not get as roiled in the spring as most lakes in other regions. Evidently, the high elevations provide a much better chance for an orderly spring runoff. By the time the ice is completely off these lakes, the angler will generally find them clear and blue. This makes it necessary generally to use lighter terminal tackle. The same applies to fishing the streams in this section during the dry summer months.

Special Pleasures

I think the angler who fishes the lakes and streams included in this section will be amazed at the beauty of these spots. The combination of rugged rock outcroppings and clear blue water in the series of lakes in Tahoe National Forest is spectacular. And when these shores are painted in a riot of color in the fall, I know of no more scenic area in the west. The same captivating scenes can be found along rivers like the Truckee and streams like those that flow into the North Fork of the Feather River. Sections of these streams, and of the North Fork itself, will also satisfy the modern angler's need to get back to a measure of untarnished wilderness.

There is a special charm, I think, to all forms of trout fishing. I even like the situation where fishing is made difficult by streamside brush, such as that found along Willow Creek. And I also like the challenge of having to fish far and fine in open pasture streams like Goodrich Creek. There is also a real challenge in fishing fast-flowing waters like

the North Fork or Truckee River or in taking trout from roadside water, as at Webber Lake. In all of these beautiful waters, surrounded as they are by pine-studded mountains or big, rock-rimmed meadows, it is a pleasure to be on the water no matter if the trout cooperate or not.

Wading Technique

Although I do virtually all of my stream trout fishing with flies and fly-fishing equipment, everything I have to say about wading technique applies to the use of other types of equipment as well. First of all, the trick to taking good trout from accessible streams like the Truckee is to fish sections rarely, if ever, fished by other anglers. Pass up sections of stream that are obviously fished a great deal. This includes most larger holes and any deep, fairly

A good selection of lures effective in fishing the high Sierra. Trout will readily hit any of these.

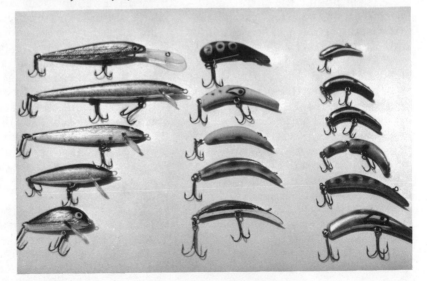

slow-moving glides and runs. Concentrate most of your fishing effort on wild white-water runs. And if these runs have large rocks and boulders, it is even better. Trout will lie in the undisturbed holes behind midstream obstructions.

These are the places to offer the trout flies, baits, or even lures. Of course, getting the lure or fly to fall deep and remain in this part of a stream is the problem, and this is where correct wading technique is important. Without proper wading, even if the cast is perfect, the fly or bait will be whipped out of the pocket before it manages to sink more than a few inches. But if you wade into exactly the right position directly downstream from a pocket, you can raise the tip of the rod and allow a fly or bait to sink deep in the pocket of dead water. The same applies when using floating flies. With the aid of carpet-soled waders and wading staff, this kind of wading and positioning is relatively simple. Without them, you can only fish the pockets from the side.

As for finding the correct wading and casting position, the shorter the cast the better. And I try to allow only the leader to touch the water. I wade until I can stand in a pocket behind a boulder downsteam and as near as possible to the pocket I want to fish. You can get amazingly close to trout in wild water, for they are not nearly as spooky as they are in more gently fllowing water. In fact, I have often looked down in fast water and seen trout right next to my leg.

Which Flies?

I did not find floating flies nearly as productive as sinking patterns for fishing the North Sierra streams in this guide. I had some success with high-riding flies like the Horner Deer Hair fly in sizes No. 12 to No. 16. But the creeks and rivers covered here are generally pretty rough flowing, and good flies like the Adams or Cahills had to be tied very heavy in order to float at all. Too, most of the streams are fairly brushy, and I chose flies that float naturally over those that had to be false cast a great deal in order to dry them. I believe you could probably do as well with a single good pattern, like a Bivisible in several sizes and colors, as you could with any other.

In choosing nymph patterns, size is critical. Make a stream-bottom check on each new stream, even those just a short distance from one another. For instance, Willow Creek has a larger caddis than does the main stream, and north fork of the Feather River, into which it flows. I found a No. 12 fly with a cream body and a sparse black hackle best for Willow Creek. But in the north fork, I had to go to a No. 16 fly with a yellow body and black hackle. Similarly, stonefly nymphs were not nearly so effective in the Feather River country as they were in the higher Sierra area of the Truckee and Yuba drainages.

I usually spend the first day and frequent periods throughout my stay examining what's available for the trout in that particular stream and in that particular drainage. One helpful method for these examinations is to use a bottle with clean water to isolate a few of the insects found in a stream. Also, whenever I am in a new area, I stop in the local tackle shops to see what local angler use to take their trout. I must admit some of the flies suggested by tackle shop operators can be bizarre. I try them and if they work, fine. If not, I go back to trying to duplicate the insects I find in the streams. I've rarely had much success with the weirder offerings, but I've got a fly book full of samples of local art.

The Leader Tippet for Clear Water

In clear waters, I consider the size of the leader tippet nearly as important as what you offer the trout. If I am fishing the Truckee, I may use a tippet of up to four-pounds breaking strength. Most of the smaller streams covered in the North Sierra section of this guide can be adequately worked with a tippet testing one or two pounds.

If you decide to use tippets tapered this small, I suggest you frequently stop to check them for knots. A light tippet is greatly affected by winds and poor casting technique. And when you throw a wind knot in a very light tippet, you have virtually no breaking strength left in the line.

I consider the leader used for clear-water fishing especially important to success. A good leader should start with a butt size about the same size, or slightly smaller, than the end of the fly line. For roughly two thirds of its length, the leader should be relatively thick, reducing in size no more than .003 for each succeeding splice.

The last third of the leader length should be short sections of monofilament that taper the leader to nearly the size of the tippet.

The way I rig my leader and tippet is to make the leader section close to 9 feet in length. I then tie on a length of tippet, usually about 3 feet long. When the selected fly is tied to the end, I make a few experimental casts. If the fly, with my particular fly-casting style, turns over too hard, I know the tippet is too short. I then lengthen it until the fly turns over cleanly and gently on the majority of casts. If the fly fails to turn over cleanly, I know the leader is too long (which it normally is with a 3-foot tippet).

In adjusting the leader, you must consider that no two flies can possibly act the same way. For instance, on the same leader, a tippet that would deliver a sparsely tied Adams on a No. 14 hook would probably require a tippet close to 3 feet to be delivered properly. On the other hand, the big Royal Coachman Fanwing has a lot of air resistance. Everything else being equal, the Fanwing would probably require a tippet close to 14 or 18 inches.

Rigging Spin Gear for Small Mountain Streams

I did quite a bit of experimenting with flies and spinning equipment while researching this guide. I figured that a fairly small percentage of readers would be fly purists, and I found flies so effective for fishing small streams, I wanted to detail the use of flies in connection with the spinning equipment used by the majority of fishermen.

One of the reasons flies outperformed lures on mountain streams is that small streams are comparatively shallow over much of their length. Even floating lures like Flatfish get continually hung up on the rocky bottoms. The same goes for natural and artificial baits, for in order to deliver baits, you have to

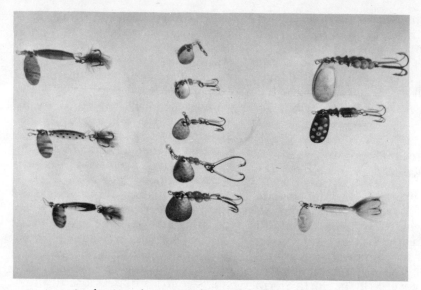

A selection of spinners that will fit the needs of high Sierra fishing. The light spinners in the center can be used effectively on even the smallest stream.

add at least a small amount of weight for casting. I repeatedly saw anglers spending more time trying to free their bait or lures from the stream bottom than they did fishing. Naturally, I didn't suggest to these anglers that maybe something was amiss. I do feel, though, that I can suggest to you readers there is a better way to go about rigging your terminal gear for fishing these small, mountain waters.

Plastic Bubble

The key to effective use of spinning gear on tiny trout waters is the plastic bubble. You can buy these in many sizes and models, any of which will do. I found the smaller bubbles, which land with a minimum of disturbance, adequate for all of my fishing.

Most anglers tie the bubble on the line above the lure or bait. But if you do this, you will miss many strikes, particularly from smaller trout, which are notoriously quick to hit and reject an offering. The best rigging I found was to tie the small bubble on the end of the line and the bait or fly about a foot up the line on a dropper strand about 10 inches long. It was surprising to me how effective this combination was. With light spinning lines, it is possible to get a very long drift that is free of line drag. And if you float a bubble downstream, you can often stay well back from the spot you wanted to fish. This is one big advantage over fly-fishing equipment that requires you to get much closer to the hold in order to fish it right. It is also a relaxing way to fish. In fly fishing, you have little chance of scoring when fishing downstream, and you are forced to fight your way upstream continually.

I experimented with both natural bait gathered from the stream bottom and with flies. I didn't keep completely accurate account of the successes of each, but there wasn't much difference between how the bait and flies performed. (By the way, most mountain streams in this guide had either caddis or stone-flies, and often both, in abundance.)

Lake Fishing

If you own a boat, trolling is probably the best way to fish any of the lakes in this section. Although the majority of trollers I saw fishing these lakes utilized metal flasher rigs fitted with either lures or bait, I have never found flashers an advantage. In fact, I think they are a distinct disadvantage in most cases. In order to fish with even the smallest flasher rigs, it is necessary to use fairly heavy rods fitted with heavier lines, usually testing around 10-pound breaking strength or more. With lines this heavy, it is impossible to offer any kind of delicate bait or smaller lure to the fish. And without adding a great deal of weight, you can't even cast baits or lures with lines this heavy.

Perhaps an outline of how I go about my own lake fishing will offer something over the usual method of trolling heavy flasher rigs. I use a

A good selection of tiny spinning lures can be used effectively on small streams. A conveniently small box is all that is needed to take them on stream or lake.

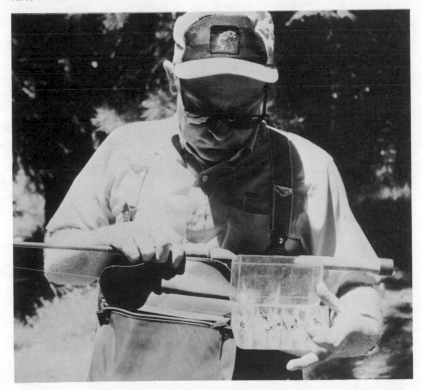

Fenwick FS 75, a 7½ foot rod that has delicate action yet enough backbone for good casting. Any rod approximately this size is suitable. With a light rod of 7 to 8 feet, fitted with a 4-pound test line, you will be ready for most situations found in the high-mountain lakes.

Timing

I try to be on the water at or near dawn when fishing high-mountain waters. I've found trout get active when the first light of day falls on the water. This is not true of every single lake every day, of course, but it is one of the rules of high-mountain fishing that I've found important. The first two hours of fishing in the morning and the last two at night are worth more than all the rest of the daylight hours put together. And in the case of brown trout fishing, this element seems to be critical.

Fishing Feeder Streams

In the morning, I normally head for the area off the mouths of live streams that feed into the lake. Even the mouths of streams that are no longer flowing during the summer and fall seem to be good gathering spots for trout. Probably the stream mouth area is attractive even when dry because the stream had dug a deeper channel in an area that is basically shallow. This makes for an ideal trout situation: deeper channel water where the trout can find sanctuary close to a food-rich shallow area.

When I get near the feeder stream, I rig with a simple spoon or wobbler. I haven't found that the type or make of the lure makes

much difference in this kind of fishing, so I've chosen the spoon or wobbler because it is the simplest kind of lure to use and the least likely to twist lines or act up in any way. I usually shut the motor off and allow the boat to drift. I cast repeatedly to the edges of the deeper channel water and allow the wind to move the boat from one spot to another.

Often, I take enough fish for a limit in the first hour or so of fishing. But I generally release these fish. In fact, I rarely keep a limit unless there is a reason. A couple of fish for eating every few days is enough to take from these fragile waters. By the way, never stay near the stream mouth or use a given method of fishing for more than an hour, at the most, if it doesn't produce trout. It doesn't really matter why the method isn't working, it's simply foolish to stick with one method or spot if it doesn't give up at least a few trout every hour or so.

Shore Casting

After the hour spent near the feeder stream, I start moving along and casting toward the shore. (I do the same in the evening.) I never see other anglers doing this, but it's a very effective way to take high-mountain trout. The best way I've found to move along the shoreline of a high-mountain lake is to put the motor in reverse and back down the length of the shoreline. By backing, you can go much slower and fish more thoroughly than if the motor is in forward gear.

I think casting the shoreline makes a lot of sense. At nearly every lake, I have seen minnows and baitfish swarming in the grasses and around the rocks in shallow water.

Good fly types are the Wooly Worm and similar patterns. These flies will take trout from any California trout area. They represent a great variety of underwater insects. Use many different sizes.

I'm sure the minnows go to these shallow shoreline areas to seek the protection of whatever cover is available. I'm also sure the gamefish in the lake know that the smaller fish hold near the edges of the lake. It is only logical, then, that the gamefish would head for this part of the lake when they decide to feed. At any rate, I always spend a part of the day fishing this area. I will change lures if they don't produce, but generally I stick with lures that are minnow-like in action and appearance.

Lake Trolling

After I've worked the shore line in the early and late hours, I usually turn my attention to trolling—the bread and butter method for most lake fishing. Trolling has a lot to offer. It is the best way to cover a lot of water in a short period of time. It allows the angler to completely control the depth at which he is working his lure or baits. In fact, the element of depth is the most important single thing the angler has to know to be consistently successful in mountain-trout fishing.

In rigging a trolling setup, I tie a dropper strand about a foot in length to one of the rings of the swivel and then tie a fairly large snap swivel to the end of the dropper. This snap should be fairly large because I will be adding additional weights to the line in order to get deeper with successive passes along the lake.

A selection of metal lures. These are the easiest of all lures to rig and use. Usually no additional weights are needed. Note the variation in size.

At this point, it is critical to determine how much line is out. Some anglers dye their line or buy colored lines. This is good if you want to take the trouble to get this kind of line. In my own case, I merely click off the anti-reverse button and back the reel off a given number of turns. A back-off count of about 30 is good enough for the first few passes. Then I start deeper trolling with a half-ounce weight on the dropper strand and a lure like a Crazy Ike, Flatfish, or Rebel. I'm not certain how deep this combination goes on a 4-pound test line with my boat and motor, but it isn't necessary to determine precisely how deep the

rig is running. The main thing is to determine which combination of line length, motor speed, and other factors are successful for that particular day of fishing.

I continue to add weight to the line about every third pass down the lake or until the combination produces. Once I find the correct combination for that lake, on that day, I am relatively certain I can take a limit of trout if I want to. The entire object in using this technique is always to be aware of exactly what combination of weights and speeds are producing. If you don't know exactly how much line you had out and what weight combination you were using, how can you return your lure or bait to that depth to take other trout?

If there are two anglers in the boat, each should troll at a different depth. For the first pass, it would be a good idea for one angler to troll with perhaps a half-ounce of lead while the other uses an ounce or three fourths of an ounce. If neither of these combinations pays off, the angler who is trolling shallower should not add exactly the same amount of weight as the other angler. Instead, he should add more weight than the other angler and leapfrog down to deeper water.

One small item that may be important to anglers who fish together often is the advantage of using identical equipment—or at least reels of the same model. I discovered years ago that I always seemed to fish more effectively when I trolled with my wife. When I was with other anglers, it took longer to figure out the right combination. I finally realized why this happened. My wife and I use identical rigs—same line, reels, rods, lures, and terminal rigs. With both rigs performing exactly the same, we could usually dope out the right combination in fairly short order. With other anglers using different equipment, it was more difficult to be exact in handling the different rigs and methods of rigging. Thus, if you troll a great deal with some other person, it may be worth it to get identical reels. The savings in time while trying to locate trout depths can be considerable.

A good selection of weights should be on hand for stream and lake fishing. Note how sinkers can be ganged on a large snap swivel for exact weight control. At right center are cloth tubes with swivels and shot inside. These are used for fishing on the bottom without snagging.

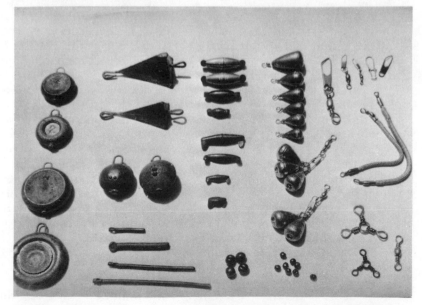

This trout was caught with a wobbling spoon lure. These are the simplest lure types to use because they require no additional weight. They are effective at any depth. When weighted they go deep because they have little drag in the water.

Summer Lake Fishing

Usually, the majority of anglers find the trout fishing "good" during the spring and early summer months, then the number of fish taken drops way down during the warm summer months. Fishing doesn't get "good" again until fall. The reason for this is that the surface water is coolest early and late in the season. During the hottest months, the waters warm and the trout generally head for the depths of the lake under the layer of warmer surface water. But the take need not drop during the summer just because the trout have gone deep to escape the warmer surface waters. In fact, the take should actually be higher in summer because the trout are gath-

ered together more than they are in the spring and fall. In the small lakes in this section, you need only follow a regular pattern for your trolling or shore fishing. Fish deeper as the day wears on. Eventually, the level where the trout are holding at that stage of the season will be found. And if you have kept track of all the elements—speed of troll, amount of line out, the weight and size as well as the specific lure you are using—you should be able to return to that depth and take as many trout as you want, day after day and season after season.

Shore Fishing

A shore fisherman is limited to the water that he can cast over; therefore his opportunities are much more limited than those of the boat fisherman. However, there are a few things the shore fisherman can do to help at least a little bit in getting better catches. One of the first things he can do is find out from other shore fishermen if they are taking trout, and, if so, where they are taking them. During the warmest summer months, trout will gang up in certain sections of a lake. Sometimes during hot weather this gathering is so tight that only a single, or a few, sections of these small high-mountain lakes will have any significant number of fish. The first job of the shore fisherman, then, is to find these spots. If no shore-fishing success is reported at a given lake, it might be a better idea to go to another lake, or to visit several before even starting to fish. A day spent driving to different lakes to determine the shore-fishing success of the anglers there is definitely worth the effort.

Successful shore fishing, like trolling, also is a matter of paying attention to detail. For example, often you'll find every shore angler gathered at the same spot and using the same baits the same way. If the other anglers are taking trout, fine; fish the same way they are. But if none of them, or only a few of them, are taking fish, it certainly doesn't make much sense to fish the same way. Why not tie on a lure and begin casting? A number of times I've found a situation where other anglers were bait fishing unsuccessfully and I've been able to take the trout by fishing with lures.

Bait Fishing

Of all the methods of catching trout,

I think bait fishing is the most restricting and the least productive for the number of fish per day of fishing. The main thing that's wrong with bait fishing for trout is that you can't cover enough water using the cast-and-sit method. Of course, this problem can be mitigated somewhat. I have watched effective bait fishermen and noted that they moved around a great deal more than less successful fellows. The successful bait fisherman is also one who checks his bait regularly and frequently. It is foolish to allow a possibly empty hook to sit on the bottom for hours on end.

A good bait angler will also equip himself with a wide selection of weights of different sizes and types and of other items like bobbers and small floats. If one method of bait fishing isn't working, it makes sense to try another. For instance, on a windy day, a lightly rigged bobber can be cast from the lee bank and the wind can be used to float the bobber out in the lake. The angler merely pulls off extra line and floats the bait out, thus giving himself an edge because he can cover more water.

One of the most effective ways to work a bait rig is to creep it along the bottom. Instead of just casting it out, propping the rod against a forked stick, and hoping a trout will come along and eat the offering, the angler who holds the rod and turns the reel very slowly will be fishing a swath of bottom from relatively deep water up through shallower water. Sure, you'll lose some terminal rigs this way; some areas are too rocky or snaggy for this method. But where suitable, this method can add a lot of fish to the creel in a season of fishing. Certainly, if one area of shoreline isn't paying off, it makes sense to move to another section. I feel certain that all shore fishermen would do much better if they moved along the shoreline continually until they begin to take some trout.

Lake Fly Fishing

I rarely see other anglers fly fishing the lakes described in this section. In a whole season of fishing, I will see perhaps a dozen anglers working the streams with flies, but lake fly fishermen seem to have disappeared from the scene. I will admit my own fly fishing in these lakes has produced less trout and generally smaller trout than are taken by other methods. But there is something soothing about flycasting in a beautiful mountain setting, that offers me something I just can't get with other types of equipment. I'm not a fly fishing snob, but I've had a fly rod in my hands since youth and I jump at the chance to do some fly work whenever I can find the right conditions.

I've seldom had good luck fly fishing when a lake is dead calm. Generally, the water in high lakes is so crystal clear, you spook more trout with a fly rig than you tempt. I usually confine my own fly fishing to those times when trout are actively feeding or when there is a slight riffle on the surface. And any time there is both a riffle and actively feeding trout, it is simple to take trout from these waters with flies.

A small selection of streamer flies should be used on these lakes. Since most of the lakes have minnows in the shallows, you should drift a comfortable casting distance off shore and work a streamer or bucktail along the shoreline. In general, I've had my best luck with a combination streamer and bucktail in which feathers and fur of drab color are mixed. However, I think just about any fly on size No. 10 through No. 16 long-shank hooks will work.

I have a collection of nymph patterns I use for all my California fishing. It represents, in general, the bug life found in our waters. However, I think that a collection of Wooly Worm flies in many sizes and color combinations would probably do about as well as anything. The trick is to allow the flies to sink deep and then retrieve them slowly, alternating jerky retrieves with slow, steady retrieves. Often a trout will follow them nearly to the surface before hitting.

Floating flies should match any hatch you see. I've rarely taken trout on dries larger than No. 14 in any of these lakes. I think an Adams, a Gray Hackle Yellow, and a selection of lightly tied Bivisibles are all you really need. Especially during the prime periods of the year, spring, early summer, and again in the fall, you will often see good trout cruising the surface. You can spot a cruiser by noting that rises occur at regular intervals along a fairly straight line as the trout moves along, usually fairly close to shore. Cast to a spot where you estimate the trout will pass. This kind of fishing is normally best at spots where a point of land juts out into the lake, for trout rarely cruise in coves. Good dry fly dope is essential, and a leader sinking compound is needed when the going gets tough. On a sunny day, a floating leader can look like a rope in these extremely clear waters.

Here the author is using an automatic reel. In some cases these relatively heavy reels are best when you have to lengthen and shorten line a lot.

Fly fishing in these waters can get very touchy. I habitually use a leader and tippet arrangement that is over 10 feet. I would say that a 12-foot leader should be standard for most of this fishing. I also use a 1-pound tippet. I've found you can handle almost any of these trout in the open waters of a lake with this size tippet.

On a few occasions, I found the only way I could take trout with flies was to troll. For some reason, a fly trolled on a sinking line and a rowed boat will tempt trout when nothing else does. A streamer fly trolled behind a rowed boat isn't very much fun, however. I usually make a long cast and then strip off extra line in this kind of trolling. I

think a big part of the success of this method comes because the rowed boat is so much quieter than a motor-driven boat. Too, it takes longer for the oar-pulled lure to pass over the fish, which may also add to the magic of this method because the trout has had a chance to settle down after the shadow of the boat has passed.

Ultra-Light Lures

In general, larger individual trout usually want something that looks like it's worth chasing before they will hit. You can try offering them some meaty looking things with fly-fishing gear, but large flies aren't as effective as tiny spinners and lures. A small wobbler is probably as close as you can come to imitating a baitfish. Also, you can offer rigged minnows on ultra-light lines with no need to add bottom-hanging sinkers to get enough weight to make a decent cast.

There are literally hundreds of different model ultra-light lures that can be used in small-stream fishing. You can hold a lot of them in a very small box that fits conveniently in a pocket of your fishing vest. For effective fishing, include several different types.

One of the most effective groups are spinners. There are many different shaped blades in the spinner group. Each has its own use and purpose. The wider blades like the Colorado spinner can be effectively used in fairly fast water. Thinner blades like the Willow Leaf can be best used in slow or still water.

With a long rod, the angler will get maximum use out of his lure collection. A 7½ ft. rod allows an angler to lift a long length of line over midstream and streamside obstructions. This means that you can sometimes use streamside brush to hide your approach, by casting over the top of an intervening bush, but at the same time, you will still be able to retrieve the lure out of the water without hanging it up in the bush.

High-Mountain Rain

If you are fishing in high mountain areas and it begins to rain, don't run for cover. Keep fishing. During a thunder shower, particularly during the first part of a downpour, trout go on a feeding frenzy. Land insects are washed into the water by the thousands and the trout know this.

Be prepared for such a helpful change in the weather (likely at the high elevations) by having a cheap plastic rain parka on hand. They fold up into a convenient package and can be stored in a very small pocket. The ones with a hood are best; those thin plastic rain hats either collect water and drop it down your neck or blow away and leave you bare-headed.

Truckee River

The Truckee River north of Lake Tahoe is a key fishery. It once enjoyed the reputation of a trophy trout fishery, but in the last few years, many anglers have come to believe the river has declined because of the easy access to it and an excessive number of fishermen. This is not so. In fact, this very belief has worked to the benefit of fishermen on the river, because it has kept the crowds away. And in the meantime, since the river's level is maintained by releases from the locks at Lake Tahoe, the Truckee has a good, year-round flow of cold water that makes for nearly ideal trout conditions.

Usually, fishing pressure is fairly heavy on the Truckee River only in the early weeks of the season. After this first flurry of activity has passed, I have found I can fish for days on end and rarely see other anglers working the river, even during the normally heavy weekend periods. Apparently, the many new

This is the prize sought by all high mountain trout fishermen. A good brown like this one doesn't come easy. They are numerous in trout waters of the high mountains, but wary.

lakes in this general area — like the Prosser, Stampede, and Boca reservoirs — have the effect of siphoning off many of the anglers.

The Truckee is a large river and only experienced and aggressive anglers can work the river to best advantage. Like many other streams in northern California, virtually every mile of the stream is readily accessible to the angler. Well-paved roads and freeway sections parallel the river for its entire length from Lake Tahoe to the Nevada border.

But if the angler tries to work the river from the roadside, he will not have much success. To reach sections of the river with good fishing, wading aggressively is the only method that pays off. If you do not wade aggressively, you cannot really sample the quality fishing to be found in the Truckee. This, of course, is true generally of any stream trout fishing. But on the Truckee River, your wading technique becomes critical.

Fishing is prohibited for the

Truckee River

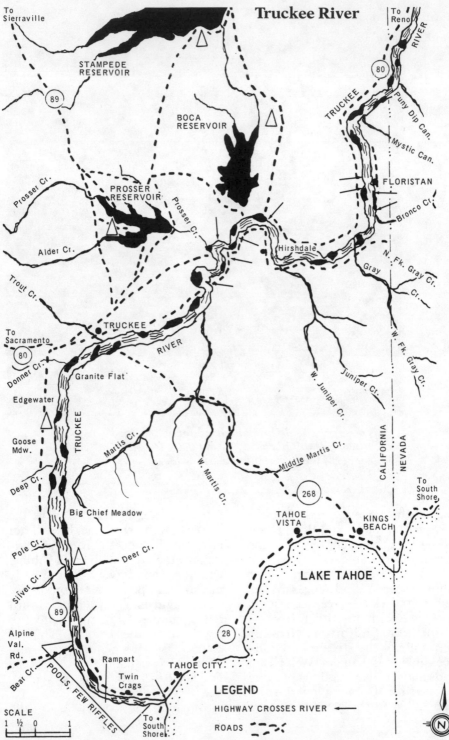

To Sierraville

STAMPEDE RESERVOIR

89

BOCA RESERVOIR

To Reno

80

TRUCKEE

RIVER

Puny Dip Can.

Mystic Can.

FLORISTAN

Prosser Cr.

PROSSER RESERVOIR

Prosser Cr.

Bronco Cr.

Hirshdale

N. Fk. Gray Cr.

Alder Cr.

Gray

Cr.

Trout Cr.

TRUCKEE

RIVER

W. Fk. Gray Cr.

To Sacramento

80

Donner Cr.

Granite Flat

Juniper Cr.

Edgewater

Goose Mdw.

TRUCKEE

Martis Cr.

W. Juniper Cr.

Deep Cr.

W. Martis Cr.

Middle Martis Cr.

CALIFORNIA

NEVADA

268

To South Shore

Big Chief Meadow

TAHOE VISTA

KINGS BEACH

Pole Cr.

Deer Cr.

Silver Cr.

89

LAKE TAHOE

Alpine Val. Rd.

28

Bear Cr.

POOLS, FEW RIFFLES

Rampart

Twin Crags

TAHOE CITY

LEGEND

To South Shore

HIGHWAY CROSSES RIVER ⟶

ROADS ----

SCALE
1 ½ 0 1

N

first 1,000 feet below the Tahoe Dam outlet. From the bridge on Highway 89 near Tahoe City, you can watch the hundreds of huge "tourist trout" feeding on items washed down to them from the lake. Beyond this area, along the upper 2 miles of the river, you'll find generally good fishing. A series of holes at and below Twin Crags and Ramparts are ideal for bait or lures. This area has never produced well for me with flies, however. Access is good, directly from the highway.

Alpine Valley Road

The next section where you will find good pocket water is at the Alpine Valley Road. Access here, about 2.5 miles from the dam, is direct from the road. You need to wade to get into proper position. The road then crosses to the west bank about 3.5 miles from the dam, and this is an especially good access point. There are several good fly-fishing sections here.

Just below this point, there is a lot of private property and the next good access is near Silver Creek campground. In summer, this part of the river gets a lot of pressure from anglers using the campground. Riffles here are relatively shallow.

Big Chief and Goose Meadow

There is an excellent rocky section of stream at Big Chief, where the river is generally wider and shallower than it is above. Between Big Chief and Goose Meadow, there is a great deal of private property and limited access, but at Goose Meadow there is another excellent rocky section. Below Goose Meadow, the river is also worth fishing if you can gain access. At Edgewater, for example, the bulk of the stream runs through posted private property, but it is an excellent section, wide and rocky. There is also some good, deep fly water where bait can be used effectively.

About 9.5 miles from the dam, you'll find a pullout where huge rocks along shore and in the river provide some fine pocket water. And a mile below the pullout, there is a rough campsite at Granite Flat, with some wide, shallow riffles. Here, I've found it best to fish along the shore where the water flows under overhanging brush.

Donner Creek

Some of the best and most accessible sections of the upper Truckee are directly upstream and downstream of the mouth of Donner Creek. The section can be located by looking for the West River street sign. There are a lot of big rocks in the stream at this point, which makes for good pocket-water fishing.

You'll find access to the river at both ends of the city of Truckee and at the bridge on the road to Kings Beach. On North Bank road, at the north end of the city, there is a selection of nearly every type of water available anywhere along the river. Even though this section is easily accessible to the townpeople, it still has some of the best fishing on the river. The road provides access to nearly 5 miles of river, although some of this area is private and posted. From the freeway, you can reach this section by taking Prosser Village Road and Forest Service road 18NO6.

Prosser Creek to Boca

One of the most productive sections on the entire river is at Prosser Creek. To effectively fish this area, however, you must either walk a long distance downstream from the town of Hirshdale or have someone drop you off on the freeway where it crosses the river (only emergency parking is allowed along the freeway). I generally have my wife drop me off when fishing this section.

At Hirshdale, the water is generally deep and strong flowing, especially when releases are being made from Boca and Prosser reservoirs. There is an ugly city dump across the river along the old highway bridge, but this area is very productive for larger trout. You should fish the white water just below Hirshdale and the large rocky bluff. In general, the north shore is best. There is a Forest Service road alog the south bank downstream from Hirshdale, but access from it is limited to only a few spots— among them Bronco Creek, which is a good area, with a lot of deep holes interspersed with riffles.

Floristan

At the Floristan off-ramp from the freeway, there are some excellent sections of white water riffles in which any type of equipment will work. The stretch below town but above the flume is especially good. Below the flume, the flow is usually very limited and the fishing is generally poor.

Farad

At Farad, the river becomes whole again and fishing is good for the next mile or so below Farad, where there are many deep holes. Access is simple from large pullouts along the highway. You'll find particularly good fishing near the railroad bridge.

The river flow is altered again below this point for power-making activities. There are side roads every mile or so in this section and an access point from the old highway that crosses into Nevada. It is hardly worth getting a Nevada license to fish this section at most times during the year, because the river diversion for both irrigation and power-making makes the fishing poor. There are some good sections below Verdi, but access is very limited.

Prosser Lake

Prosser Lake, a few miles north of Truckee, is a typical high-mountain reservoir—about 140 feet deep, a surface area of 754 acres when full, and ideally located for trout fishing at just over 5,700 feet. The elevation of lakes like Prosser is especially important to quality trout fishing. With any lake located at elevations of 5,000 feet or more, the weather is such that water temperatures near the surface warm slowly in summer and cool quickly in the fall. This means trout will be near the surface for a much longer period of each year than in lakes at lower elevations.

There is a good paved launch ramp near the campground at Prosser which will accommodate a boat of any size. However, since the camp facilities are located away from the water's edge, anglers using the camp must take their boats out of the water each night. There is also a smaller campsite at the west end of

Dave Terri with breakfast trout he caught at Prosser Lake.

the lake where your boat can be left safely in the water.

I have had my best luck at Prosser trolling around the edges in the spring and fall with near-surface lures. You'll find rainbow trout primarily, but there are also some good brown trout. The area near the inflow of Prosser Creek is one of the top spots for fishing. In the fall, brown trout gather there waiting for water levels to rise so they can go upstream to spawn. And in the spring, rainbows gather here getting ready to spawn. In fact, rainbows are usually spawning in Prosser and Alder creeks when the stream-fishing season begins in the spring.

In August and early September,

I've found it's necessary to troll deep. The best spots at Prosser are near the outlets on the northeast and the south end of the dam, where there is a deep trench that attracts huge concentrations of trout. Shore fishermen can easily work this area.

There are some rough camping areas along the north edge of Prosser. The best access to this end of the lake is from old highways and roads that were there before the lake was formed. One top spot for both camping and fishing is at the northeast end of the dam, where the spillway is located.

Fishing in Alder Creek is good only during the spawning and runoff periods. Most of the year the

Prosser Lake in late fall. The water is drawn down at this time of year. In spring after runoff, the lake extends almost to the camera.

creek doesn't carry a significant head of water. There are some campsites along Alder Creek.

Prosser Creek

Prosser Creek, above Prosser Lake, is a beautiful trout stream. Even in the warmest summer months, the stream runs cold—an ideal 55 degrees. The lower part of Prosser Creek is accessible off Highway 89 at the upper end of the lake. This section of the creek has a fair head of water except in the very late part of the season and is fairly good fishing. To reach the upper sections of Prosser Creek, where the fishing can be ideal, turn west at the road south of Alder Creek.

The north and south forks of Prosser Creek can be reached by turning north off Alder Creek road onto 18N12. The south fork is a beautiful little mountain stream where the road crosses it. There is a lot of ideal pocket water here. Because of a big burn, many trees have fallen into the creek to provide excellent hiding spots for trout. In addition, the creek is typically rocky, and there are many waterfalls with good numbers of trout sheltered below them. The typical trout from this section was 9 to 13 inches.

The north fork of Prosser Creek

is another important stream for trout. The banks are wooded and access is limited to a few spots where minor roads lead from the main road to rough campsites near the water's edge. The upper section of the north fork is heavily posted private property.

The north and south forks of Prosser Creek join a short distance below where the Forest Service road crosses the south fork. Because of the additional water from the joining forks, fishing in this part of the stream is very good. Fish taken below the junction will generally be larger than those above. There is also less streamside brush, in general, in the section below the junction. Good wading conditions are available along the whole length of the stream.

I've found the fishing best near the area where the two forks join, and I've had my best luck with small No. 14 lures and smaller nymph patterns (I checked out the underwater food supply and found plenty). The water is very clear, which means that you should use as light a terminal rig as you can handle. If you hook larger trout, the light leader will make for sporty fishing.

Boca Lake

Boca Lake is much the same as Prosser. The spillway is 5,600 feet and trout-fishing conditions are ideal. Access to the lake is good along the west shore, where there are launching sites and an intricate road system. Most roads lead to rough waterside camps, and you can fish ef-

Crystal clear streams like the Rice Branch of Prosser Creek can often be fished best by an angler kneeling. Low casts are also a good idea, where possible.

fectively from the bank anywhere along the entire shoreline. Be warned, however, that Boca has no speed regulation, so skiers will usually be on the water during the warm weather months.

A paved road heads along the east side of the lake to the headwaters of the Little Truckee River. One of the best spots in the area to fish is near where the Little Truckee enters Boca Lake. The same conditions occur here as at the mouth of Prosser Creek on Prosser Lake.

Stampede Lake

Stampede Lake, located at an ideal 5,900 feet, is probably the most pro-ductive of the three reservoirs discussed so far. The lake was formed by flooding a relatively flat meadow, which means that the water covers large areas where food can be produced on a massive scale. Since aquatic growth can be produced only in areas where sunlight can reach the bottom—normally a depth of 20 or 30 feet in these clear-water areas—the shoreline depths at Stampede are very productive, particularly along the north shore.

At Stampede I've found no particular spot where the trout seem to gather. The area near the dam outlet attracts brown trout when the reservoir is spilling, and a natural gathering spot for Stampede Lake

Boca Reservoir, one of the oldest in this part of the high Sierra. Some really nice trout, browns and rainbows, are found in Boca. Fishermen will find water-ski competition in summer.

fishing is where the Little Truckee enters the lake. Sagehen Creek is another good spot, except that the flow in the Sagehen is relatively limited. For trolling some of the best spots are near the dam and the smaller side dams.

There are excellent camping facilities and launching sites on the south side of the lake, and an extensive road system services the north side of the lake. You can enter the water in this area by using the old roads that led into the now-flooded meadow. There are also many rough campsites on the north and west shore.

Sagehen Creek

Sagehen Creek is a tiny stream with a fair head of water. Located above Stampede Lake, it can be reached from Highway 89 on side roads that follow both banks of the creek. Sagehen is a very brushy, weedy creek and in most areas it can only be fished with bait. It is an interesting stream to fish because you have to get so close to the fish before you can deliver an offering. In the middle section of the creek, there is a posted, half-mile university test section where no fishing is allowed.

Little Truckee River

The Little Truckee River, between Webber Lake and Stampede Lake, is a tricky stream to fish. There are some fair-sized trout in this river, but getting them out is a chore. In the upper reaches of the Little Truckee, access is mainly limited to steep banks. A few sections can be reached where unpaved side roads cross the river. These feeder roads head off the Henness Pass road,

which is paved. One good fishing spot with such an access is at the bottom of a huge box canyon that you can see from the main road. There is also some brushy bait-fishing water nearer Webber Lake that is worth fishing.

The stream flow has been altered by a diversion dam a short distance below Webber Lake, so there is barely enough water between the diversion dam and the mouth of Independence Creek to maintain a fishery. Below Independence Creek, however, the Little Truckee is a typical meadow stream with a fair fishery, much of which is located on private property. Some nice trout can be taken from the Little Truckee in this area if you can gain access. Most trout on the Little Truckee are fairly small— a 10-incher would be a big fish from these waters.

Independence Creek

Independence Creek, which is maintained year-round by flows from Independence Lake, supplies most of the water for the lower stretches of the Little Truckee. About the only way you can fish the bulk of this creek is with bait poked through the brush. But this is a good little creek for the bait fisherman; there are some surprisingly good trout. Many sections flow through relatively flat ground where the current has gouged out ideal holding pools and undercut banks. It's challenging to try to sneak a bait successfully into these spots. There are some rough campsites along the creek.

Independence Lake

Independence Lake has some good

Little Truckee Region

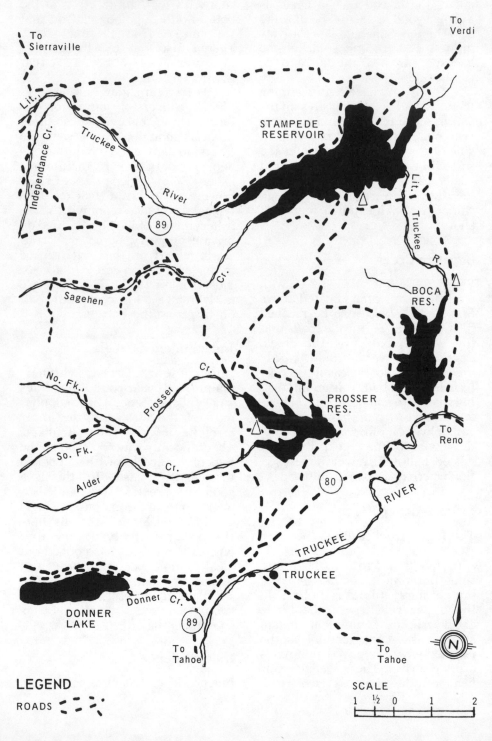

To Sierraville

To Verdi

Lit.

Independance Cr.

Truckee

River

STAMPEDE RESERVOIR

Lit. Truckee

R.

89

Cr.

Sagehen

BOCA RES.

No. Fk.

Prosser

Cr.

So. Fk.

Cr.

PROSSER RES.

Alder

To Reno

80

RIVER

TRUCKEE

TRUCKEE

DONNER LAKE

Donner Cr.

89

To Tahoe

To Tahoe

N

LEGEND

ROADS

Two cutthroats from Independence Lake. These cuts are a prize in California waters. Originally their range was large but they do not compete well with other introduced species of trout.

rainbow and cutthroat trout fishing. The cuts have gone as big as 12 pounds, but most will be much smaller. This very scenic lake is owned by a power company, which charges for camping. The best spots to fish are along the south shore and near where the creek enters at the southwest end. Another good spot is near the outlet when they are releasing water.

Webber Lake

Webber Lake is one of the finest of the fishing lakes found in this part of the mountains. It is noted for larger brown and rainbow trout. There are wide areas of food-producing shallows that keep fishing quality high, and any method of fishing can be used effectively here. I have found, for example, that you can troll a fly effectively in Webber Lake. Perhaps one of the reasons that this method is effective is that so few other anglers fish this way in this hard-fished lake. Trolling is the most commonly used technique at Webber Lake.

A few mornings, when trout were feeding actively on the surface, I also took good trout, mostly rainbows, by casting flies. I haven't seen many anglers scoring regularly by bait fishing from the shore, but bait fishing can be good near the inflow from feeder streams. The best spot for this is at the southwest corner of the lake. The feeder streams

Casting flies or lures from the lakeshore is often more effective than trolling or boat fishing. Here Pat Freeman is unhooking a trout from Webber Lake.

virtually all dry up in the fall and late summer.

Webber Lake is one of the first lakes in this area that you can reach after the snow is off the ground. You'll find it by taking Henness Pass road off Highway 89. A fee is charged by the owners of Webber Lake for camping and for fishing from a boat.

Lake of the Woods

The name, Lake of the Woods, aptly describes this beautiful little lake. It is an alpine jewel. It's not very big, just a few acres in extent, and it's mostly shallow. However, the center of the lake is deep enough so that trout have a year-round sanctuary from warm surface water. The trout are small, but they are colorful natives. Lake of the Woods can be reached by a wide and extremely steep road through heavy forest. This road is so steep that you would be wise to wait until it is dry before traveling it.

Early and late in the season is the best time to fish this lake. And to fish it right, you really should have a boat (a motor is not necessary). Fish near the outlet on the south end of the lake, where a small bog is formed. In this area, I think that you could effectively use any lure, but one that acts like a frog was very successful for me—probably because there are literally thousands of tiny frogs in the boggy areas around the lake.

I also found fishing around blowdowns near the edge of the lake a good bet. Shore fishing is limited, because only at the north end are you able to cast into deep water from shore.

Yuba River Region

Jackson Meadow Reservoir

Jackson Meadow is a relatively new lake, built in 1965 and filled even later, with 11 miles of shoreline and a surface area of 1,000 acres. I found fishing in this lake unsettled; the planted fish haven't yet settled down to any sort of pattern.

The area near the feeder streams produced well in the spring and fall, and the spillway, at 6,000 feet, should make for ideal trout fishing. However, every time I have

Meadow Lake in late fall. This scenic lake is one of the highest in this area. It can be fished near the surface even in summer.

fished this lake, there has been a lot of water manipulation, which, perhaps accounts for the strange behavior of the trout. When I used my electronic locating equipment, I found concentrations of trout at 40 feet one day and 10 feet the next, even in hot weather.

Jackson Meadow is typical of most mountain lakes in that fishing is best early and late in the season. There are many campsites at the lake. Henness Pass road crosses the dam, but it is unpaved on the west side at the present time.

Middle Yuba River

An area of excellent fishing often overlooked by anglers is the Middle Yuba River below Jackson Meadow dam. The river here flows through a deep gorge for about 1.5 miles before it runs into a regulator lake, Milton Reservoir. There are some very fine sections of wild white water as the Middle Yuba runs down this steep slope between the two reservoirs.

I hesitate to tell readers to wade in this section because stream flows can be changed at any time. However, in my own fishing, I have never been bothered by changes, and the Middle Yuba is so productive in this section that is certainly worth working even if you don't wade. You should also try fishing the Middle Yuba just about Milton Lake, where the river flows through relatively flat ground and has formed a brushy meadow stream complete with undercut banks.

Milton Reservoir

Milton Reservoir is a gem, a larger

Lake of the Woods. Located at 5,700 feet and maintaining a constant deep level, this regulator reservoir is also very good fishing. You don't really need a boat to fish this lake. Where the Middle Yuba pours into the lake, you can fish from the shore. The currents here are strong and the water is cold and well aerated from the flow from Jackson Meadow. The trout in Milton are very well fed and will bite very selectively. There are several rough campsites at the east end of the lake in a grove of trees.

Meadow Lake

Meadow Lake is an excellent choice for fishermen during the warmer parts of the summer months. It is located at 7,400 feet, where the water will remain cool near the surface longer than in most high-mountain lakes. If you are pulling a trailer or have a big camper, take the road into Meadow Lake from the Henness Pass road to the north. An alternative route up from Jackson Meadow is rough at the present time and steep for many miles.

Trolling is excellent at Meadow Lake almost all the time. Trout will be found all around the shoreline, and shore fishing can also be very good early and late in the day during the summer months. Early and late in the season you can fish effectively any time of day. There are many rough campsites on the west side of the lake.

French Lake

French Lake, which sits in a magnificent, high rocky basin, is a very pretty lake. I didn't fish this lake be-

*Milton Reservoir where the middle fork of the Yuba River enters.
This is a beautiful setting and usually is not crowded.*

cause access is limited by private ownership. The lake is a domestic water supply and no camping is permitted.

Catfish and Tollhouse Lakes

Another private lake is Catfish Lake, on the road between Jackson Meadow and Meadow lakes. The shore is posted against camping, but a small area where you can park is located off the road. You really need a boat to fish this lake because the shoreline is brushy and the water is weedy.

Another tiny lake, Tollhouse Lake, is located just to the east of Catfish Lake. Here, too, you really need a boat; even trolling is limited due to underwater weeds. The road

is rough into this whole area, but it is still passable to autos and pickup trucks.

White Rock, Fordyce, and Sterling Lakes

White Rock Lake is a very scenic lake, but only anglers with a four-wheel-drive vehicle can reach it. I didn't fish this lake, but anglers I talked to said it was very good. I know from personal experience that Fordyce Lake is one of the most productive lakes in this entire area. However, the road from the south or north is rough even for a jeep. You really need a boat to fish Fordyce effectively. At the east end, where the inflowing creeks are lo-

*Middle fork of the Yuba River below Jackson Meadow dam.
Note the plume of white water at right center where water
booms out of a big pipe in the face of the dam. The short stretch
of river below the dam is excellent.*

cated, fishing is good all season, even for fly fishermen.

Lake Sterling is another that is rough to get to. The road into it is passable to a pickup. There is a Boy Scout encampment at the lake, but during the fall you can use the few rough campsites at the lake's edge. About the only time you will have trouble taking trout here is when the water level is rising or falling sharply. It is best to fish from a boat. There are so many snags and stumps around the shoreline that shore fishing is tricky. Even trolling, except in the center of the lake, is very difficult.

Fordyce Creek

Fordyce Creek is one of the most productive I found in this entire region. I fished it in the early fall and late summer, when most streams in the area were warm and not very productive. Fordyce, however, delivered some excellent trout.

I found Fordyce almost by accident when checking out Eagle Lakes. (I found them very poor, by the way — really just big weed beds.) The road in is very rough, though I did see another angler who made it into the trailhead at the creek crossing in a pickup with a four-speed transmission. The road ends at the creek trailhead and there are a few rough campsites nearby.

Each time I've fished Fordyce, I found it with an amazing head of water, far more than any other stream in this area except the Truckee River. But since the creek is used by water manipulators for transfering water from higher elevations to Lake Spaulding, I don't know how much flow is on hand year-round. It may be cut to a minimum during some periods of the year.

I found it best to follow the creek on foot for a considerable distance downstream and then fish back upstream. There is every type of water from deep, blue-green pools to wild white water cascading over bedrock. There are even some sections that are beaver swamps.

I have little doubt Fordyce Creek ranks as the best or near the best of all the streams in this section of the Sierra. The access point to it is from Indian Springs campground off old Highway 40, now replaced by Interstate 80 at Indian Springs.

South Fork Yuba River

The south fork of the Yuba River is in general a gin-clear section of water between the headwater at Soda Springs and Lake Spaulding. The river twists and winds around the Interstate 80 freeway, which makes it easily accessible to fishermen.

There is a great deal of private, posted property along the river. Access is best along the sections fronted by the abandoned Highway 40. The best area I found was downstream from Indian Springs.

I also discovered that when you can find hard-to-get-to spots, the river will give up fair trout. Most of the trout I took came from the fast-moving sections of the stream. And I saw bait fishermen doing fairly well in deep pools. I suspect many of the trout I took and saw taken were planted fish. They generally ran about 9 inches, seldom larger.

Below Lake Spaulding, the south fork is much reduced in flow. There is still enough water here to support some fishing, however, and I saw fishermen regularly working. Below the dam and the road leading to Bowman Lake from Highway 20, there are some very deep pools, suitable for bait fishing.

Lake Spaulding

Lake Spaulding is one of the most accessible of all the lakes in this area. It also has an excellent boat launching facility and campground. Trolling is the best method of taking trout here. I tried casting for my fish with lures and flies but failed to score, even when I fished as close to the fast water at Fordyce Creek as I could get.

In the summer, Lake Spaulding is generally good fishing because the inflow of water is nearly constant and the continual inflow and outflow keeps surface temperatures lower than in most of the lakes. Usually, you can fish near the surface at Spaulding until some time in August, when the trout go deeper to escape the higher surface temperatures. The best spots I found at Spaulding were near the mouth of Fordyce Creek and the south fork of the Yuba River.

Fuller Lake

Fuller Lake is not too productive for the shore fisherman, but trolling is

South Fork of the Yuba River Region

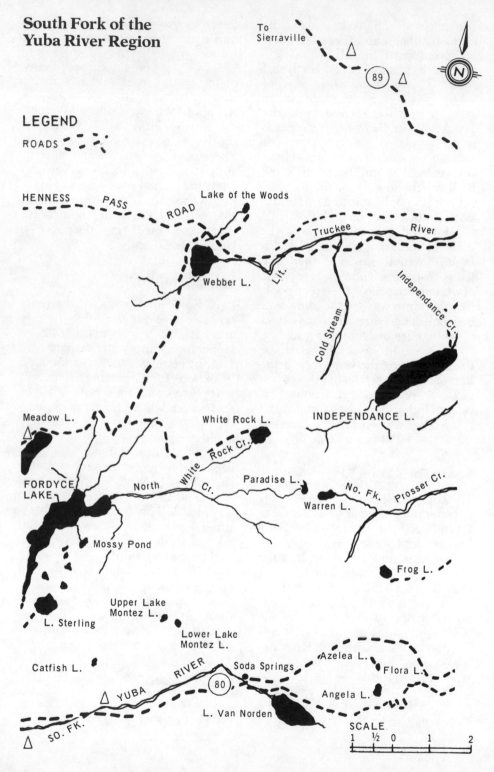

To Sierraville

89

N

LEGEND
ROADS

HENNESS PASS ROAD

Lake of the Woods

Truckee River

Webber L.

Lit.

Cold Stream

Independance Cr.

Meadow L.

White Rock L.

INDEPENDANCE L.

White Rock Cr.

FORDYCE LAKE

North

White Cr.

Paradise L.

Warren L.

No. Fk.

Prosser Cr.

Mossy Pond

Frog L.

Upper Lake Montez L.

L. Sterling

Lower Lake Montez L.

Catfish L.

YUBA RIVER

Soda Springs

Azelea L.

Flora L.

80

Angela L.

SO. FK.

L. Van Norden

SCALE
1   ½   0   1   2

Good campsites are scattered throughout the scenic lake country of the high Sierra. They are crowded only two months of the year.

good all year. Fishing the edges of grass beds is especially effective. Early and late in the season, the trout work these edges, and they can be easily taken with flies. Deep trolling is not generally necessary. The best spots seemed to be near the inflow pipe and near the dam. I also found trolling about 10 feet deep off the face of the dam very effective. There's a small campground at the lake, and the road is paved to the site.

Rucker and Blue Lakes

At Rucker Lake, summer access is somewhat restricted by a Girl Scout camp. During the rest of the year, however, this lake can be conveniently fished. You really need a boat to fish Rucker efficiently because of the shallow water and the grass beds along the shore. Shore fishing is only so-so, even before the grass grows up during the warm months.

You need a jeep to get to nearby Blue Lake, but it's worth the effort and time. This is an ideal little mountain lake. A boat helps for fishing success.

Fall Creek

Fall Creek is one of the few streams in this part of the forest that has a fair head of water in it throughout the year. The creek is brushy, and bait is about the only way you can work it. There are some excellent, deep holes, and small trout can be taken by floating a bait under the overhanging brush.

Carr Lake

It's definitely worth making a trip to the string of small lakes from Carr to Round Lake. You can drive to Carr Lake in any car or pickup, but the road is passable only for a Jeep at the east end of Carr Lake.

The best place I found on Carr Lake is near where the creek flows into it. In the morning and evening, surfacing fish gather here almost every day of the season. The rest of the lakes in this chain are typical high-elevation trout waters. A boat is not essential but it helps to have one. Even a raft is a help. It is irksome to see trout dimpling the surface in an unreachable portion of the lake.

I've had very good luck with No. 14 Mosquito pattern flies at Carr Lake. Of course, this is a good pattern for fishing just about any of the waters in this section. Another good pattern is an Adams, in sizes No. 14 through No. 20.

In these high-mountain waters, hatches can come off the water at any time of the day; and as the sun reaches down through clear water, it often triggers some remarkable hatches. Trout are very selective during these feeding sprees. It really puts the fisherman on his mettle to score when trout are feeding avidly on a single type of insect.

Flume Fishing off Bowman Lake Road

You can sample a unique form of trout fishing in the flumes found in this area. Actually, between Bowman Lake and the Yuba River, these flumes contain virtually all the flowing water in the area. Still, I've seen very few other anglers trying this game.

There are miles of open flumes which you reach by way of the many service roads that head west from the Bowman Lake road. These flumes are just ditches cut along the side of the mountains. The downhill sides of these ditches are mostly concreted to hold the water, which flows at a very fast pace. The uphill side of the flumes is normally just the natural earth and rocks.

Trout would not survive long in these fast-flowing canals if they couldn't find some kind of cover. This they seek on the uphill side of the flume, where they find rocks and other obstructions. Every time you find a fair-sized rock, you'll also find a good trout.

The way I fish these flumes is to walk the downhill edge of the flume and cast across to the more sheltered uphill side. I cast a fly or lure, even bait, and then merely walk along with the offering until it has had a chance to sink deep enough to almost touch the rocks of the uphill bottom. Generally, you can't fish from the uphill side because trees and brush come to the water's edge.

The trout found in these flumes evidently don't have a good diet. Although some of them are fairly large, I've found they are not very fat. Of course, this may also be because life in the flume's fast waters makes the fish more streamlined than regular stream trout. In any case, I've never found trout more willing to take a fisherman's offering than those in the flumes.

Lindsay Creek and Texas Creek

The lakes and streams in the Lindsay Creek and Texas Creek chain are ideal trout waters. The best way to fish these lakes is to treat them as a chain and fish the higher elevations as the season progresses. In the higher lakes, most trout are brookies, while the lower lakes hold good rainbows.

Lindsay Lake is located at 6,200 feet and can be reached readily with a pickup. With careful driving, you can also reach it with a car during most of the season. The same is true of Lower Rock Lake, but only a four-wheel drive vehicle can get to Upper Rock Lake or Upper Lindsay. Though all of these lakes can be fished from shore, they are best fished from a boat.

Texas Creek is fishable with bait, with the best fishing below Bowman Lake road, where the stream has been joined by Lindsay Creek and has gathered size. Access to Texas Creek is rough but worth the effort. The ideal spot to fish is at the bottom of the access road that ends at the flume. You'll have to scale down a steep bluff, but there are some beautiful, deep pools formed where the creek cascades over a series of rocky ledges.

Bowman Lake

At Bowman Lake, the primary problem faced by the angler is access. Most of the shoreline is so steep you can hardly stand up, let alone launch a boat. However, in periods when the lake is full, a boat can be launched at the north end. At this north end, a huge flow of water pours into Bowman from a big tunnel that cuts through the mountain all the way from the Middle Yuba. Fishing seems to be best at Bowman where the tunnel empties into the lake. Evidently this inflow provides a large amount of food. The same is true at the upper, eastern end of the lake, where Jackson Creek enters. However, during the fall, Jackson Creek barely flows.

In general, Bowman Lake contains larger fish than most of the high-mountain lakes in this section, except for Webber Lake. I think there must be a very fertile underwater growth to account for the size and good condition of Bowman trout. Also, there is a lot of water manipulation in this entire basin, and the continual rising and falling of the water may allow a high yield of insects. I've found fly fishing better at Bowman than at any other lake other than Fordyce Lake. However, the best method to fish here is still trolling, with the upper end ideal.

McMurray Lake

McMurray Lake, at 5,900 feet, is very scenic and fairly productive. It offers a few campsites and a lot of good minnow activity among the shoreline grasses. You can launch a boat at the point where the road passes the lake.

Weaver Lake

Weaver Lake is one of the best lakes in this area, but you need a boat to work it properly. The last hundred yards of access is especially difficult and unless you have a four-wheel-drive vehicle, you will have to carry a boat for a considerable distance to get to the water. The effort is worth it, however.

Bowman Lake Region

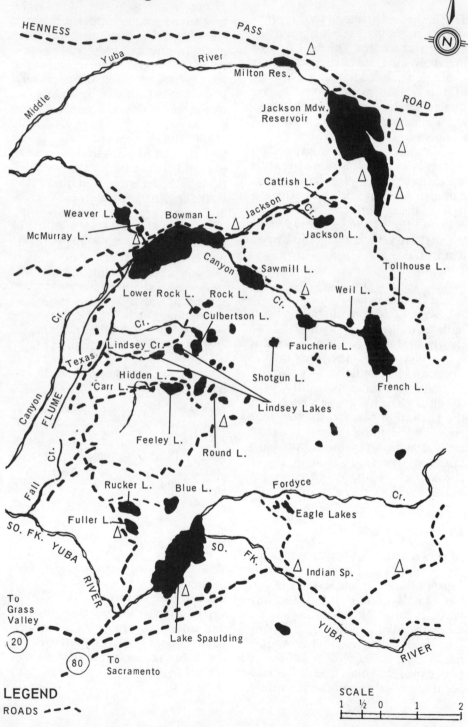

LEGEND

ROADS – – –

SCALE
1 ½ 0 1 2

Sawmill and Faucherie Lakes, Canyon Creek

In the Canyon Creek drainage, there are two excellent lakes, Sawmill and Faucherie. At Sawmill, located at 5,800 feet, you can launch a boat near the dam. Shore fishing is good in the few spots where you can gain access.

Faucherie Lake is an extremely scenic and productive lake. Most of the trout I took from this lake were small, but the exciting scenery, with massive rock headlands and sparse shoreline vegetation, is worth the trip regardless of your catch. There is a good picnic facility at the lake, and shore fishing conditions are excellent. You can launch a boat at the dam by crossing the dam.

Canyon Creek is best fished at the big pools just downstream from Faucherie dam. For most of its length, the creek is so brushy it can only be fished with bait. There is an excellent campground between Sawmill and Faucherie lakes.

North Fork of the Feather River

I have included some of the trout waters of the Feather River in this guide because I felt that there are a significant number of fishermen who prefer stream fishing to lake fishing. In general, in California, there is no shortage of excellent trout lake fishing. In the case of stream fishing, however, there has been so much damming that good trout streams are getting harder to find all the time. Some of the best still remaining in California are in the north fork drainage of the Feather River.

These streams are all relatively easy to get to, which is important, especially to anglers who don't have a lot of time to fish. But despite the fact that these waters are readily accessible, they don't seem to be fished much except in the immediate environs of road crossings or large campgrounds.

The north fork of the Feather is a fairly large stream, even in the low water period of autumn. It is not as big as the Truckee; but as more and more creeks flow into it near Lake Almanor, you can always depend on a good head of water. In fact, some of the most surprising and gratifying fishing in California can be found in the city limits of Chester and in the lower sections of the river. To protect this high quality fishery, the state keeps the north fork closed an additional month each year, so that rainbows that have come upstream from Almanor will have a chance to spawn. (The migration of brown trout normally takes place after trout season is over, but some years, good browns can also be taken from the north fork the last month of the season. I don't think the brown trout fishery is much hurt by taking spawners, so long as anglers replace the female browns, which you can tell by their lack of the distinctive upward curve in the male lower jaw.)

The majority of creeks in the north fork drainage are spring fed. This is important to summer fishing success, since during the hot sum-

North Fork of the
Feather River Region

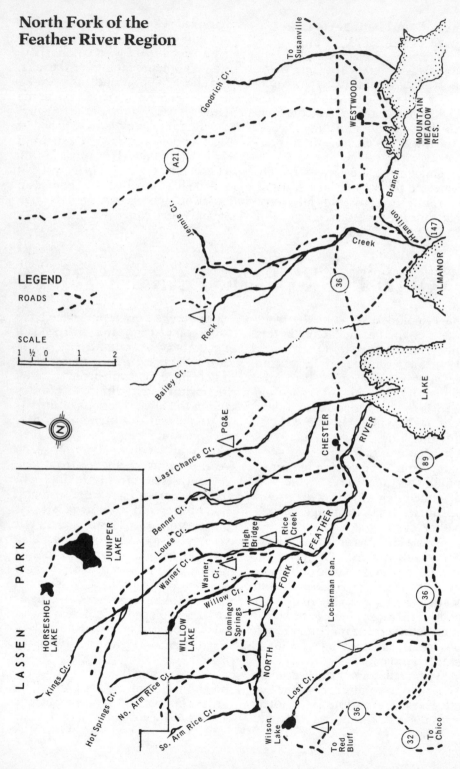

LEGEND

ROADS

SCALE
1 ½ 0   1   2